# FOUR SEASONS OF CARP

**W**elcome to Four Seasons Of Carp – over 100 pages filled with all manner of carp fishing stories and features for you to enjoy.

Each season is covered and some of the country's very best carp anglers share their knowledge with you. As well as relaying their tales of successful sessions, they also offer plenty of tips for you to take away and catch more carp for yourselves, whatever the time of year.

So, whether you're a hardened, 12-months-of-the-year carper or even if you prefer to go fishing only when the sun is shining, there's plenty in here for you.

I have to admit that work commitments during spring and summer mean that most of my fishing is done nearer the end of the year, a time when, for me, our countryside, including fisheries, is at its finest and most alluring.

I've spent many an autumn night admiring my surroundings, and soaking it all in. The deep red skies, which are so 'big' at this time of year are a joy to behold. Also, I reckon that most waters' carp are in the very best condition throughout the autumn months. All of this combines to make this magical time my favourite period of the year.

That said, no season can match the excitement that spring bears. As many anglers dust off their gear and the carp begin to wake from their winter slumber, spring is a time when we all become more active. With rod licences, and vigour, renewed many carp anglers make their way to waters up and down the land in a spring assault.

Whatever your favoured period, I hope you enjoy reading Four Seasons Of Carp and that it inspires you to get out there and catch more carp.

**Marc Coulson**
**Editor, Total Carp**

# CONTENTS
## FOUR SEASONS OF CARP

Published by David Hall Publishing Ltd. The advertisements and editorial content of this publication are the copyright of David Hall Publishing Ltd and may not be quoted, copied or reproduced without the prior permission of the publisher.

Copyright © 2008

Compiled and edited by Marc Coulson
Layout and design by Katie Wright and Nicola Howe
Sub edited by Lee Jones
Reprographics by Thomas Webb and Stephanie Horn.

# SPRING

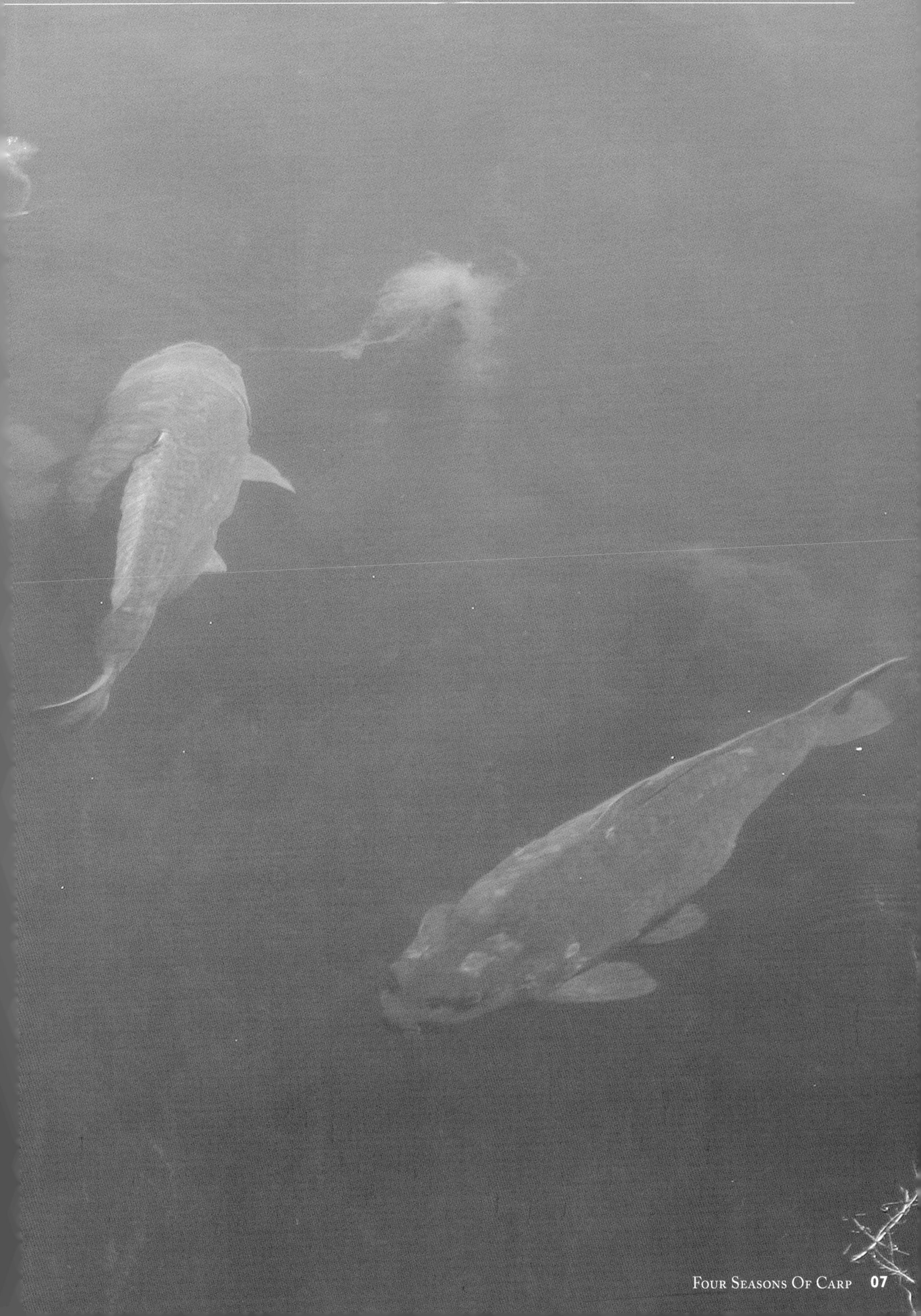

# SEVEN JOBS FOR SPRING

With carp, and carp anglers, waking from their winter slumber, MARC COULSON and JON BONES highlight important tasks that are undertaken before they start fishing.

It's that time of year again when we all seem to blow away the cobwebs and put our carp fishing heads on. Okay, we have all been out doing plenty of short-session winter trips, but now is the time when the rest of the gear comes out and we start to think about carp fishing proper.

Spring represents a real watershed in our carp fishing years and it's now that the preparations begin for some full-on carp fishing. Preparation is everything and there are always a few jobs that need to be taken care of before the 'season' gets under way.

Here, Marc and Jon explain what those important tasks are and how we go about making sure that they are sorted before we start fishing in earnest.

Check them out, there may just be one or two things that you could do with following. Good luck…

## ENERGISE YOURSELF

Replace, or at least check, the batteries in your alarms, receiver and headtorch. If they have been in storage over winter then it's likely that they will have deteriorated. You do not want your batteries to die on you mid-session – take it from us; it's a real pain in the proverbials.

If you always take a gas stove with you then make sure that your gas bottle has plenty left inside it.

A gas bottle that's almost empty takes an age to boil a kettle and if you can't make tea then you might as well go home!

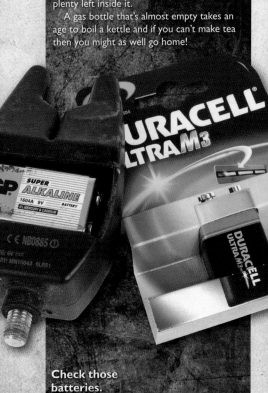

Check those batteries.

## CUT IT OUT

Jon is known for taking as little as he can get away with on most sessions, but it's a bit different for our editor. Marc tends to take a few more luxury items in the cold wintertime, but these are ditched for the season ahead. Marc says that the majority of his fishing this year will take the form of quick overnighters, as family commitments mean that he has to be at home more. Taking the bare minimum will help him set up quickly and pack away at the last possible minute, before leaving to return to work the next morning.

Marc can get everything he needs into his rucksack and quiver.

## BAIT UP

Now is the time to visit your water and start introducing a bit of your chosen bait. By giving the fish some of your freebies on a little-and-often basis, they will start to recognise it as a valid food source. Take it from us, time spent doing this now can bring you rewards throughout the rest of the year.

Now is the time to start trickling your bait in.

## TICKETS PLEASE!

The one thing that you must do is renew your Environment Agency rod licence. Remember, one licence covers two rods, so if you fish with three or four rods you will need to buy two licences.

As well as the rod licence, this time of year often represents club/syndicate-ticket renewal time. Marc has a period from late January through to May when all of his tickets come up for renewal. It takes him all the previous year to save up for them! Don't get caught short without your tickets – renew those that are due.

## GET SEARCHING

With the carp moving about more they're easier to spot. If you can find them then you can catch them. Get down to your chosen water and start looking. Find them now and you will build an idea of their spring and summer haunts. Do not underestimate the importance of time spent looking for carp before fishing.

**Always take care when tree climbing.**

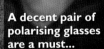

**A decent pair of polarising glasses are a must...**

**...and binoculars are also handy.**

## SURF THE NET

Fishery websites and forums will be awash with catch reports from now on. Study them closely, decide which waters are 'on form' and then get down there to cash in on the action. As well as websites, check out the weeklies. Carp-Talk magazine is a great place to find out which waters and regions are starting to turn on.

Jon recommends always keeping an eye on the weather forecast – the Internet comes into its own here, too. It'll put you in the box seats when the right conditions arise because you know what to expect. JB frequents all sorts of sites (ahem) including *www.metcheck.com* and *www.bbc.com/weather* to stay in the know.

**Check out the weeklies and the Internet for news of fish captures.**

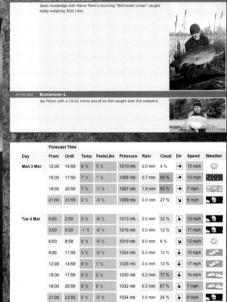

| Day | Forecast Time | | Temp | FeelsLike | Pressure | Rain | Cloud | Dir | Speed | Weather |
|---|---|---|---|---|---|---|---|---|---|---|
| | From | Until | | | | | | | | |
| Mon 3 Mar | 12:00 | 14:59 | 6 °c | 3 °c | 1010 mb | 0.0 mm | 4 % | → | 15 mph | |
| | 15:00 | 17:59 | 7 °c | 1 °c | 1008 mb | 0.7 mm | 95 % | → | 10 mph | |
| | 18:00 | 20:59 | 7 °c | -1 °c | 1007 mb | 1.9 mm | 93 % | ↘ | 7 mph | |
| | 21:00 | 23:59 | 0 °c | -3 °c | 1009 mb | 0.0 mm | 27 % | ↘ | 6 mph | |
| Tue 4 Mar | 0:00 | 2:59 | 0 °c | -5 °c | 1013 mb | 0.0 mm | 32 % | ↓ | 10 mph | |
| | 3:00 | 5:59 | -1 °c | -6 °c | 1016 mb | 0.0 mm | 12 % | ↓ | 11 mph | |
| | 6:00 | 8:59 | 0 °c | -5 °c | 1019 mb | 0.0 mm | 8 % | ↘ | 12 mph | |
| | 9:00 | 11:59 | 3 °c | -2 °c | 1024 mb | 0.0 mm | 10 % | ↓ | 15 mph | |
| | 12:00 | 14:59 | 8 °c | 1 °c | 1028 mb | 0.0 mm | 13 % | ↓ | 17 mph | |
| | 15:00 | 17:59 | 6 °c | 2 °c | 1030 mb | 0.2 mm | 77 % | ↓ | 16 mph | |
| | 18:00 | 20:59 | 6 °c | 0 °c | 1032 mb | 0.2 mm | 67 % | ↓ | 7 mph | |
| | 21:00 | 23:59 | 0 °c | -3 °c | 1034 mb | 0.0 mm | 24 % | ↘ | 6 mph | |

## CHOOSE YOUR WEAPONS

Jon uses the uneventful late-winter period to roll and cook up some 'special' hook baits. If you haven't already done this, but want to, then get busy. Make sure you roll enough for the entire season.

Now is also the time that Jon chooses, and stocks up on, his chosen bait. It is best to decide on a bait and stick with it. This allows you to build your confidence in it and also buy it on a regular basis in order to compile stocks.

**Choose a bait that you trust and stick to it.**

**Jon will have all his hook baits sorted by spring.**

# PVA Bags Made EASY

JON 'Shoes' JONES reveals a great spring tactic that is both easy to use and catches loads of carp.

There are seldom many products launched these days that can really revolutionise the way that we fish certain tactics or methods. However, every now and then there is something that you look at and think: "Oh yes, that's a winner."

That's exactly what I thought when I saw the Quick Change PVA Bag System from Solar.

The idea was spawned, I guess, from Rob Maylin's revelation of the mag-aligner rig and the way in which he fished it to catch carp using large, web-type bags of PVA filled with maggots. Basically, Rob's rig was a helicopter rig with a swivel and quick-change clip at the end of the leadcore leader. The PVA bag was attached to the clip before being cast out into the swim, complete with a maggot and plastic maggot combination hook bait.

The method soon took off and many a top angler now employs it on waters where maggots work well.

I've seen a dedicated version of this rig, with all the components, for sale commercially recently, but I did always think that the system could be slightly easier to use.

It seems that Solar thought exactly the same and, with the launch of this system, it has made the maggot-bag tactic easy for all to use. It's also cut out one or two of the rig components, meaning that there is much less metalwork on display in the set-up.

By introducing a dedicated steel clip, which replaces the insert of an inline lead, Solar has done away with the need for the quick-change clip. A simple tail-

Maggots are great but the rig works with most baits in a PVA bag.

Inline leads are a must for Jon's rig.

rubber-type item tidies everything up and then it's fished pretty much the same way as Rob intended.

I don't want this feature to sound too much like an advert – and I am not sponsored by Solar as some of the cynics among you might suspect – so that's

enough of the product itself, save to say that everything you need to fish this rig is included in the pack.

So, how and when would you use this system? Well, the first thing I would say is that you needn't be blinkered into thinking that it's only any good when

## HOW TO USE JON'S SOLAR BAG SYSTEM

**1** All of the components you need are in the packet, except for the inline lead.

**2** Remove the plastic insert that comes in the inline lead. This is a Korda Flat Pear.

**3** The new Quick Change System Clip will replace the lead insert.

**4** Jon favours either Solar's looped leadcore leaders or a Korda Safe Zone leader.

**5** Thread the leadcore through the lead and onto the Quick Change clip.

**6** Pull the Quick Change clip into the lead so that it sits flush, as shown.

**7** Next, thread the tail rubber onto the leadcore leader and pull it down, like so.

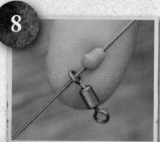

**8** Follow this with a rig swivel and one of Solar's new Leadcore Backstop Beads...

**9** ... which are really versatile and can be used for loads of different presentations.

**10** This is how the rig looks so far. It's dead easy to set up and takes seconds.

**11** We are sure that this system is going to be extremely popular.

**12** Tie your chosen hook link to the swivel and you're ready to attach your PVA bag.

# ATTACHING YOUR PVA BAG – IT'S SIMPLE

**1** Pull the Quick Change clip from the bottom of the inline lead, like so.

**2** Clip your stocking-type PVA bag onto the loop in the Quick Change clip.

**3** Now, pull the clip back inside the lead, trapping the bag in place. Brilliant!

**4** Nick the hook into the side of the bag, making it neat and tidy for casting.

fishing with maggots. I have been using it with pellets, boilies and all manner of baits. It does work best, however, with the stocking-type PVA, so some finer ingredients won't work unless you dampen them for use in the bag, such as groundbait.

Because every man and his dog seems to write about the mag-aligner and fishing with maggots, I deliberately used the system with pellets and boilies. This was purely to show how versatile it is – in the same way as PVA-bag fishing is. That said, if you choose the right water, using the system with maggots is absolutely devastating.

The sequences of step-by-step instruction shots depict perfectly how the system is set up and you will hopefully see how easy it is to use. However, and more importantly, it takes seconds to attach a new bag and recast it to your spots.

**Maggots can be used easily...**

**... in these spods, with their solid inserts.**

This constant recasting to your areas is a good way of keeping the swim topped up, especially if you are using maggots. I like to spod the odd load of maggots over the top on a regular basis too. It's important that you use a spod with solid sides (or tape up the holes) when spodding maggots, or you'll lose half of them in the process.

People are often saying that using maggots can be expensive, especially when using this style of fishing, which requires a lot of bait. However, most tackle shops will sell you a gallon (eight pints) of maggots for around £16. This will last you a day session, if not a little longer, so it's only like getting through 1½kg of boilies. Nevertheless, on the right day, it will get you a hell of a lot of bites and you will be glad that you made the effort.

**Jon's favoured hook-bait arrangement.**

**A Todber Manor twenty falls for Jon's spring approach.**

# IT'S A BITE

The weather's improving, the carp are on the feed and it's time to start catching. We send ELLIS BRAZIER and IAN DAY out to cash in on the springtime action…

L et's face it, the winter months are miserable. The long hours of darkness, the awful weather and the lack of carp activity don't make for exciting fishing. Still, that's all behind us now and it's time to get back out there and get a bend in the rod.

For a bit of enthusiasm, and a few tips of course, we asked Ellis Brazier and Ian Day to nip out and bank a few fish for the cameras. They both duly obliged and met on the banks of an old sand pit in Shropshire. Having fished here several times over the past three years, Ellis knows a little about the place and brings both Ian, who has never been here before, up to speed.

"The lakes holds around 60 carp up to 28lb," says Ellis. "The water consists of a thin channel with two mouths, one on either side of the lake, and a main body of water of about two acres. The shape of the lake can make it difficult to find the fish, but if you do find them they are very catchable. I came down a few days ago on a recce session and bagged eight carp in just a few hours."

Ellis' recce trip threw up a few doubles like this one.

After a quick wander up the bank and a discussion, Ellis settles into a swim at the end of the channel, just into the main body of the lake.

"The margins are the most productive areas," explains Ellis. "By targeting the mouths of the channel, the plan is to pick the fish up as they move in and out of the main body of water. The third rod I'll cast about in open water."

Ian has headed 40 metres up the bank to the far end and set his gear down in the last swim. The water in front of him is sheltered from the wind by a huge

Slack lines as Ellis keeps it subtle.

Ellis fires a rig to a channel on the far bank.

Simple tactics, but they prove fruitful.

You won't miss this bailiff!

sand pile from the working quarry next door. As a result, it's flat calm.

"The wind is cold and 'stale' because it's been blowing in the same direction for days," says Ian. " I'm hoping that the carp have moved up into this sheltered water where it's slightly warmer."

Both anglers sort their gear and soon have their rods cast out. Like Ellis, Ian is targeting the margins. One rod is cast tight to the bank on his left, one is cast tight to the far margin and the third is dropped off an overhanging tree to Ian's right. Rather than complicate things, Ian has opted for a D-rig presentation with a critically balanced hook bait on two rods and a 2ft zig rig on the other.

"For extra attraction I've scattered a few Sonubaits S-Pellets around the zig

rig," says Ian. "The oil that these pellets emit will create a column of attraction in the water, adding that little extra to my approach."

Targeting the channel on the opposite side of the lake means that Ellis has a line stretching the width of the lake. By fishing a semi-slack line he's looking to pick up line bites, giving him an indication that carp are in the area. With his right-hand rod, Ellis is casting straight past an inlet pipe to the mouth of the channel on his side of the lake. Inlet pipes are often exceptional features and well worth fishing near, but Ellis has chosen to ignore it for good reason.

**Inlets can be great features.**

"This pipe is fished all the time, it's probably the most pressured area of the lake," says Ellis. "The inlet is constantly pumping water into the lake, so it loses its impact/attractiveness as the carp become used to it. Don't get me wrong, in the warmer weather the carp do frequent this area because of the cooler, oxygenated water being pumped in, but it's not the one today."

The morning wears on with no sign of fish. Nothing is seen and neither angler receives any indications. Ian recasts the rod on the far margin further along the bank, to a gap in the trees. He goes on to explain that recasting regularly

**Attract the smaller fish and the bigger ones often follow.**

# ELLIS' MULTI-ATTRACTION BAG MIX

**1** Ellis uses crushed hemp and pellets and an 'active' feeder mix.

**2** Tip equal quantities of both groundbaits into a clean bucket.

**3** The key ingredient is a mixture of crushed pop-ups.

**4** Next, add a few tutti frutti and pellet-flavoured dumbbells.

**5** The juice from a tin of sweetcorn and a few of the golden grains are added.

**6** The next ingredient is 2mm Sonubaits Feed Pellets.

**7** Finally, Ellis adds a quarter of a tub of Tuna Dip.

**8** Give the ingredients a thorough mix. Leave to stand for half an hour.

**9** There you have it, a bag mix that will attract carp from all around.

when you're not getting any action is important.

"You have to remember that the water is still cold, despite being sat here in glorious sunshine," says Ian. "When the water's cold the carp will be very localised and unlikely to move far to investigate or pick up your baits. You therefore have to search them out."

With no action to speak of, Ellis sets up his stalking rod and drops it into the margins of the little lake directly behind him. This lake is full of carp, although they only go up to about 12lb, so it's a safe bet for a take or two. Minutes later his alarm bursts into life and Ellis is soon posing for the camera with a small common.

Hooking a small PVA bag of multi-coloured bag mix to his fined-down rig and small hook bait, Ellis flicks his rod back into position in the little

**Ian has brought some new hook pellets...**

**... as well as Tutti Frutti and Pineapple Wraps to try out.**

lake. With that sorted he explains his bait choices while they await the next take.

"I like to add movement to my baits," starts Ellis. "Carp anglers are far too static. Their approach is static and their baits are static. By adding a visual stimulant to your baits you give them

Action from the runs water for Ellis.

## IAN'S SPRINGTIME TACTICS

**1** Ian chooses a critically balanced pineapple hook bait and a D rig.

**2** This is coupled with a lead-clip set-up. Note, Ian's trimmed the clip.

**3** A length of ESP Anchor Rig Tube complete's Ian's set-up.

an extra dimension and appeal to more of the carp's senses. I put a mixture of different flavoured and coloured pop-ups, which I've put through a blender, into my bag mix. This adds plenty of colour but the various-sized pieces of pop-ups rise through the water at different rates, adding movement to the mix too.

"You might have noticed that my hook baits are somewhat smaller than a standard 14mm-boilie approach. I've spent a lot of time watching carp feed and I've seen them treat whole boilies with caution. They'll pick up a boilie, back off from the feed, spit it back out again and really play around with the bait before eating it. On smaller food items, such as particles, the carp simply come in and devour the lot. They feed with far more confidence on small baits, maybe because it's far closer to their natural diet of tiny food particles than a bed of boilies."

The bobbin on Ellis' middle rod, the one cast to the channel on the far side of the lake, pulls right up to the rod butt before dropping back again as he receives a savage liner. The severity of the liner leads Ellis to believe that a fish hitting the line quite close in caused it. His third rod, the one in open water, is wound in and dropped short.

Further up the bank, Ian is playing around with a few of Sonubaits' baits that he's brought along. He's been trying out the Tutti Frutti and Pineapple Boosted

Wraps as both hook baits and feed, and has also tried some Bacon Grill, Paste Pellets. As we discuss the baits Ellis wanders up the bank and informs us that he's caught another little common on his 'snide' rod. They're stood behind Ian's swim looking across the water when a carp, a decent-sized common, sticks its head and shoulders above the water, just 20 yards out. Ian quickly winds one of his rods in, attaches a PVA bag of three Pineapple Wraps and flicks it out to where the carp showed. Having seen a fish, and knowing that at least a few of them are on the move, the lads' spirits are instantly lifted.

Unfortunately, the action doesn't materialise and Ellis is stood in his swim an hour later. The 'snide' rod does the business once more and Ellis bags another small common. He unhooks

and returns it just as Ian shouts down the bank. The main lake has produced the goods, but surprisingly the bite didn't come from the area where the carp showed. The bait cast tight to the far margin did the business and Ian is soon posing with a double-figure common. It's a very clean fish, in that there are no leeches or lice on it, which would suggest that the carp has been 'laying up'. It's a good sign because it means that the carp are probably active.

With the pictures taken and the fish returned, Ian casts his rod back to the far margin. He then reels in the rod he dropped short and fires that across to the far margin too, alongside an overhanging bush.

"Where there's one carp, there are usually more," says Ian. "With two rods in the productive area I should increase my chances."

With Ellis due to be on duty that evening, he's a fire fighter, it's time for him to pack up and head off. Ian decides to stick it out until dark, but no more action is forthcoming.

... another little critter for Ellis.

A welcome double caught tight to the far margin.

# SUBSCRIBE NOW!

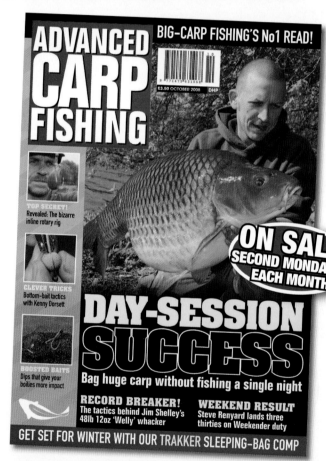

# GET THE BEST OUT OF...
# PARTICLES

TOM DOVE reckons that spring is the time to break out the particle baits and start catching carp. Here, he reveals exactly how to do just that...

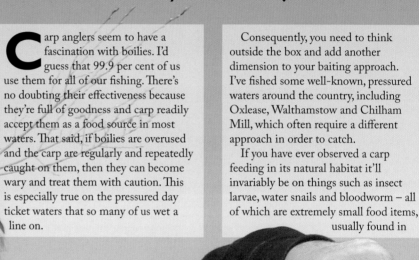

Carp anglers seem to have a fascination with boilies. I'd guess that 99.9 per cent of us use them for all of our fishing. There's no doubting their effectiveness because they're full of goodness and carp readily accept them as a food source in most waters. That said, if boilies are overused and the carp are regularly and repeatedly caught on them, then they can become wary and treat them with caution. This is especially true on the pressured day ticket waters that so many of us wet a line on.

Consequently, you need to think outside the box and add another dimension to your baiting approach. I've fished some well-known, pressured waters around the country, including Oxlease, Walthamstow and Chilham Mill, which often require a different approach in order to catch.

If you have ever observed a carp feeding in its natural habitat it'll invariably be on things such as insect larvae, water snails and bloodworm – all of which are extremely small food items, usually found in

Four of Tom's favoured particle hook baits.

weed or silt. I'm sure that the reason why particles work so well is because they resemble these small, natural foods.

A particle generally falls into three categories, a nut, seed or a pulse. Hemp, sweetcorn, tiger nuts, peanuts, tares and maize are just a few of the more popular particles. Maggots are a great addition too, although they're not strictly particles, as long as there aren't too many roach and perch in the water that you're fishing.

Hemp has to be one the most successful particle baits ever used. It's full of natural aromas, oils and resembles a water snail perfectly. This is due to its size, dark colour and crunchy texture. I tend to use hemp when fishing over weed, but only in small amounts. If you introduce too much on a session then the carp can become preoccupied, which will severely decrease your chances of a pick-up.

Dry your particle baits before using them in PVA.

A mixture of baits is best.

# HOW TO MAKE TOM'S PARTICLE MIX

**1** Add a good dose of prepared hempseed. Carp absolutely love this stuff.

**2** Follow this with a particle mix. This adds various sized and shaped baits to the mix.

**3** A sprinkling of tiger nuts is the next ingredient, but don't add too many.

**4** Finally, add a couple of handfuls of broken boilies. Job done – get out there and catch some carp!

Due to the tiny size and oil leakage of hempseed, you can often induce the carp into a feeding frenzy where they tear the lake bed to pieces searching out every last grain. If you find yourself in this situation then your best bet for getting a take is to present the matching particle on a rig, a Bogey rig for example, or simply put three or four grains on the hair. I'll go into more depth later in the feature.

Tom despatches a small bag of tigers to his baited spot.

## TOM'S TIGER-NUT PRESENTATION

**1** These are the components needed for tying this rig.

**2** Carefully bore a hole two-thirds of the way into a tiger nut.

**3** Cut a small cylinder of cork to fit snugly in the hole in the nut.

**4** When mounting the nut on a rig, go through the cork and nut, like this.

**5** Take a length of supple braid. Tom favours Korda Supernatural.

**6** Tie a small hair loop in the end of the braid, as shown.

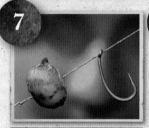

**7** Thread the hook bait and hook onto the braid.

**8** Tom ties the hook on using a KD knot – a slight variation on the knotless knot.

**9** Tom has absolute faith in the effectiveness of the finished rig. He's caught loads on it.

To avoid the problem of preoccupation I ensure that I use a mixture of particles. My usual mix contains Bait-Tech's Parti Mix, sweetcorn and crushed tiger nuts. Using a mixture of baits means that the carp feed on a variety of different sized, shaped and flavoured items and don't become preoccupied with one bait. When using nuts I fish them in halves or chopped into irregular shapes. This is to steer away from regular-shaped baits, which carp can associate with caution at times.

One thing that I'm a bit particular about is ensuring that my hook bait acts in the same manner as my free offerings. The hook will weigh the

hook bait down if you simply thread it onto the hair. As a result, this bait will not behave the same as the free offerings, which may cause the fish to eject the bait on picking it up or avoid it altogether.

To balance a tiger-nut hook bait, I drill out the core of the nut using a specially designed nut drill and insert a cylindrical piece of cork. The buoyancy

of the cork counteracts the weight of the hook, ensuring that the hook bait acts as naturally as possible. The other advantage of a critically balanced hook bait is that it can be sucked back into the carp's mouth easier than a standard bottom bait because it's lighter.

Tiger nuts are a cracking bait on waters that contain an abundance of crayfish. Their tough outer shell, the nuts' that is, will withstand the attentions of crayfish, for a while at least.

Kryston Bogey is a product that I've been playing around with, which is designed so that you can use tiny particles as a hook bait. It's an ultra-sticky, clear resin that has no aroma. By wrapping the resin around an 8mm cork ball and placing dry seeds onto it, you can form a particle ball that can then be used as a hook bait. I usually mount this on a soft hair with a split shot below it on the KD rig. The rig can then be coupled with a bag of PVA-friendly particles or a bag of dried hemp, which I dry

The best way to bait up with particles.

Tom's favoured attack is a tiny bag of tiger nuts.

Bait spoons are great for short range introduction of particles.

A small spodful can be enough to switch the carp on to your particle baits.

off using a hand towel.

The main problem that anglers encounter when using particles is how to introduce them. The easiest and most common way of feeding them is via a spod. Depending on the distance that I'm casting, or the size of particles that I'm using, I will choose one of three spods. On small waters, where I want to keep disturbance to a minimum, and at short range, I opt for the Korda Mini Skyliner. If I need to spod at medium to long range then a Korda Skyraider is more suitable because it's larger and is designed for distance casting.

At extreme close range, when targeting carp next to marginal snags or bushes for example, I prefer to introduce particles via a baiting spoon. It's a very quiet way of placing particles accurately and is especially useful when a stealthy approach is needed. You can place literally anything into a baiting spoon, from boilies to particles to liquids. I even drop my rig into position using a spoon, again to keep disturbance minimal.

When fishing over sweetcorn, my choice of hook bait is one or two grains of imitation corn. This ensures that nuisance fish can't whittle away the bait and steal it from the hair. As with the Kryston Bogey rig, I will mount the corn on a KD rig with the shot on the hair.

I've just about run out of space, but before I go I'd like to note some of my most memorable particle captures. I had

## A HUGE AREA OF BRIGHT-YELLOW CORN LYING IN CLEAR WATER IS TOO BLATANT.

Sweetcorn is another favourite particle bait of mine, but only in small quantities. I don't use large amounts because a huge area of bright-yellow corn lying on the bottom in clear water is far too blatant and is an obvious danger signal to the carp. Nonetheless, I like to have a spread of kernels on the lake bed so that the carp have to search out each one.

a cracking season on the Essex Manor, where I tempted a fish known as The Anchor at 40lb, as well as the sought-after Northern Linear at a magnificent 41lb. Both of these fell to corn and lupins, proving that particles aren't just a small-fish tactic – big carp also love them!

Don't ignore the margins.

Proof that small baits catch big carp.

# Summer

Small but perfectly formed.

Great carp in wonderful surroundings.

# CARPING IN PARADISE

Marc Coulson joins NEIL SMITH as he makes the most of a chance visit to a breathtaking venue where all your carp fishing dreams could come true...

The famous 'Koi' at around 18lb.

A cracking common at 22lb 6oz

The fish known as Five Star at 25lb 3oz.

For several weeks the trip to Rob Hales' Monument Lake was at the front of our minds. With all the gear loaded into the vehicles, Neil, our friend Steve Grace and I arrived at the Shropshire venue only to find that disaster had struck.

This ill fate was ours and certainly not the carp's – they'd started spawning and we were treated to a fabulous display of sexual gymnastics by 30lb and even 40lb carp, right beneath our feet in the lake's margins.

A great sight maybe but we couldn't possibly fish for these carp. They had much more important things on their minds. It was then that our luck turned when Sam the bailiff said that Rob had given us permission to go and fish at Weston Park instead. We'd all heard how terrific Weston was, but none of us had experienced the place for ourselves. Nevertheless, we were extremely excited at Rob's generous offer, so Sam led the way as we made the short distance to our new venue.

Driving through the gates we are greeted by a sight similar to something out of The Secret Garden. Huge trees stretch into the clear blue sky, while rhododendrons show off their purple bloom all around us. Without wanting to overstate things, it was close to breathtaking in the very literal sense of the word.

I remark to Neil and Steve that it is simply the most stunning lake that I have ever visited; and I have been to a few nice ones in my time. Neil agrees that seldom has he found somewhere so stunning to wet a line.

Weston Park is a hugely impressive stately home-type affair set in rolling Shropshire countryside and boasting this stunning lake at the boundary of its grounds. For those of you that are into your music, Weston is the venue for the annual V Festival and attracts many visitors all year round.

However, it's the fishing that we are here for and after a gentle tour of the lake Sam bids us goodbye as we unload the gear from Steve's van. As Neil and Steve set up in their swims I have a wander along the margins in search of carp. With the polarising glasses on it's easy to find a few clear spots in the weed. I chuck a handful of hemp on to one and when I return a couple of minutes later there are carp on it. Neil pops around with a rod and flicks a rig perfectly on to the spot.

"It's really important to check out the margins when you first arrive at a lake like this," Neil explains.

"It is very quiet, with only two or three anglers up the other end, so the carp feel comfortable in the edge. I reckon they look well catchable too, but I fear that one chance is all we might get. Once you've caught one the others tend to spook away. So, it's a good idea to try and bag one early doors."

Bang! As Neil and I whisper on the bank a carp rips into Neil's bait and nearly pulls his rod in. After a decent battle the fish is soon in the net and Neil is smiling for the cameras with the first carp of the day. It's not the biggest fish in

Neil recommends four-bait stringers…

… fished over plenty of boilies.

the lake, but we always take pictures of the first one, just in case it's the last!

We wander back to Neil's swim and get around to the job in hand. His rods are set up for The Monument and this lake is a different proposition altogether. Whereas The Monument is an open, clean-bottomed pit, Weston is more intimate and very weedy – although it has been treated recently and is largely in retreat.

"I need the lead to come off the clip in the event that the fish finds the sanctuary of the weed beds, so making sure that the swivel stays put is vital. These pins work brilliantly, but I wish the companies that make them would supply plenty of spares because I am always losing them!" he tells me.

As we sit and look at Neil's set-up, Steve wanders round to tell us that he's just lost one in the weed. Bizarrely, given

All of the Weston fish are in good nick.

## YOU NEED A REALLY GOOD HOOK-HOLD IN THESE WEEDY CONDITIONS.

So, off come the helicopter rigs and long-range leads and on go some lead clips and smaller, flatter leads, ideal for the weed and silt in Weston. Neil is using the Fox lead clips that feature a small pin to make sure that the swivel stays put inside the clip itself.

our topic of conversation just now, Steve explains that his swivel had come out of the lead clip, causing the lead clip and lead to jam in the weed while the fish continued to take line through it. This is exactly the problem with some lead clips that Neil was referring to.

Neil finally gets his gear sorted and casts two rods to a huge, clear strip the other side of the weed bed in front of him. He then uses a combination of catapult and throwing stick to deposit 1kg or so of boilies over the top.

"Rob Hales told me that these fish adore a bit of bait, so I've put some in to gauge

their reaction. If they come on it and I start catching a few I'll keep topping it up. You cannot take out what you've put in, though, so I've only started off with half a kilo over each rod," Neil explains.

Neil's third rod is cast tight to a gap in the rhododendrons on the opposite margin, where he has seen a few carp show themselves.

Neil tells me: "I nipped round a few minutes ago and put some bait in the margin and there were carp on it within minutes. Consequetly, I'm going to flick a baited rig into the gap from my swim and see how we go. Sam said that this is a great swim and that this spot in particular produces a few fish, so it has to be worth a try."

A couple of casts later (I'm being kind – it took Neil ages!) and he has the spot sorted as his rig flies right into

All the Weston Park swims have a net, sling and mat.

Steve Grace bags the trip's biggest fish at 32lb.

the spot. Neil's concerns that the number of casts he needed may have spooked the fish are unfounded because, while he sets his bobbin, the rod tip slams round. Fish on!

The carp gives Neil the right runaround and he almost loses it in the weed. He eventually has it nearing the net but cannot gain any more line as the weed has jammed in his tip ring. As he brings the rod down I manage to clear just enough line for him to bring the carp to the waiting net.

"Get in!" he proclaims as he looks down on what appears to be a nice fish.

At 22lb the common is the biggest of the trip so far. That is until Steve enters the swim with news of an even bigger one waiting in his landing net. It pings the scales round to 26lb and is a great start.

Over the next couple of hours both anglers experience some pretty decent action. Steve's rods see regular bites and he soon notches up eight fish. There are none bigger than the 26-pounder, but all are very clean, pretty fish. Neil's open-water rod soon begins to produce too,

and after five rapid bites he tops the swim up again with boilies.

"The fish are obviously on the bait and I want to keep them here for as long as I can. Another half kilo of boilies over the top should keep them occupied.

"I have lost a couple of fish too, and my hook-holds were a bit precarious on two of those that I landed. This is a bit of a problem because you need a really good hook-hold in these weedy conditions. However, I've switched to a double-bait rig and they seem to be nailed a bit firmer. It's more of a mouthful for the carp to try and eject and can often lead to better hook-ups. I haven't lost one for a bit so I think that it's done the trick.

Take care, as weed can jam in the tip ring when playing fish.

Neil's winning rig components.

Strong gear is needed on weedy lakes.

The Weston carp were attracted to the splash.

Feeding the swim from the far margin.

Neil keeps the swim topped up with bait.

There's no real pattern to when the bites come. One minute a rod will rattle off. Then we might be waiting a little while for the next bite and two will come at once. It's a terrific venue and we agree that it's well worth a trip. You fish in wonderful surroundings and there's a great chance of a few fish.

"It's not just the tricky casting at night. Some of these carp have dashed straight into the trees and small, snaggy bay to my right and I really don't fancy my chances of getting them out in the night. I won't risk the fish's safety either. It takes me that bit longer to get to the rods during the night and they could

and one that seems really overlooked these days.

"Spraying a few boilies about and fishing stringers over the top has caught me no end of carp and it's a brilliant method on boilie-dominated waters such as this one," he continues.

Now, I won't have it said that I am a heavy sleeper and I certainly do not snore (my wife will tell you otherwise). Nevertheless, the next morning Neil and Steve insist that they were unable to rouse me from my slumber when they caught carp. Each has caught a couple more in the night, including a twenty apiece.

## NEIL FOLLOWS WITH LATER ON WITH ONE OF THE LAKE'S FAMOUS RESIDENTS, FIVE STAR.

It's now 7pm and Sam returns with a curry from the local takeaway.

The action is so frantic by this stage that both Neil and Steve wind in their rods so that we can eat without interruption. A couple of bottles of lager help the food down nicely and what is already a great trip just gets better by the minute.

Neil decides that he is only going to cast two rods to his open-water spots for the night because he doesn't want to risk too may miscasts to the tight spot on the margin area.

make the sanctuary of the snags. I simply feel more comfortable not fishing there," he explains.

He does make the time to go round and put some more bait over the margin spot, in the hope that there will be carp there in the morning. Meanwhile, he attaches a couple of stringers to his other rigs and casts them the 60 yards or so to the open-water spots.

"That will do. I reckon they'll be worth a bite or two in the night. Have you noticed that I'm on the stringers again mate?" Neil asks. "It's a fantastic tactic

"You were too busy snoring fella. It sounded like a herd of buffalo rampaging through the swim. I thought it best to let you enjoy your kip!" Neil jokes.

They didn't bother with pictures either – we'd already agreed that we had enough shots in the bag and night shots wouldn't be necessary unless one of the lads caught a real whacker.

With the rods wound in we take the time to have a look around the wonderful boathouse at Weston, which

## SLIP 'EM BACK SAFELY

**1** Neil returns his fish to the water on the unhooking mat or in the sling

**2** One last picture before this scraper twenty is returned safely.

**3** He holds the fish in the water for a minute or two so that it recovers its strength...

**4** ... before allowing it to gently slip back into its watery home.

Neil lands a ball of weed... with a carp in it!

Accuracy is the difference between bites and blanks.

Take your time when casting into small holes

can be booked by anglers for a week at a time. In fact, the entire lake is soon to be available to book individual swims on a weekly basis. I speak to Rob about getting in early because I have no doubts that this place is going to be immensely popular.

It's soon time for me to make my way home, but the guys are staying on for a few more hours in a bid to wait for the M6 to calm down. They're both glad to have done so as well, because over the next few hours they both continue to plunder Weston's bounty.

Steve texts to say that he's landed a real lump at 32lb and Neil follows later on with one of the lake's famous residents, Five Star, at just under 26lb. The pair finishes with more than 30 carp between them, including several big twenties and a thirty.

All of this in a fabulous setting and with all the modern facilities that we carp anglers crave.

Is there a better place to go carp fishing and enjoy great surroundings with the real chance of a personal best carp? If there is, then I certainly haven't been there yet.

Neil's efforts are rewarded with this great, 28lb common.

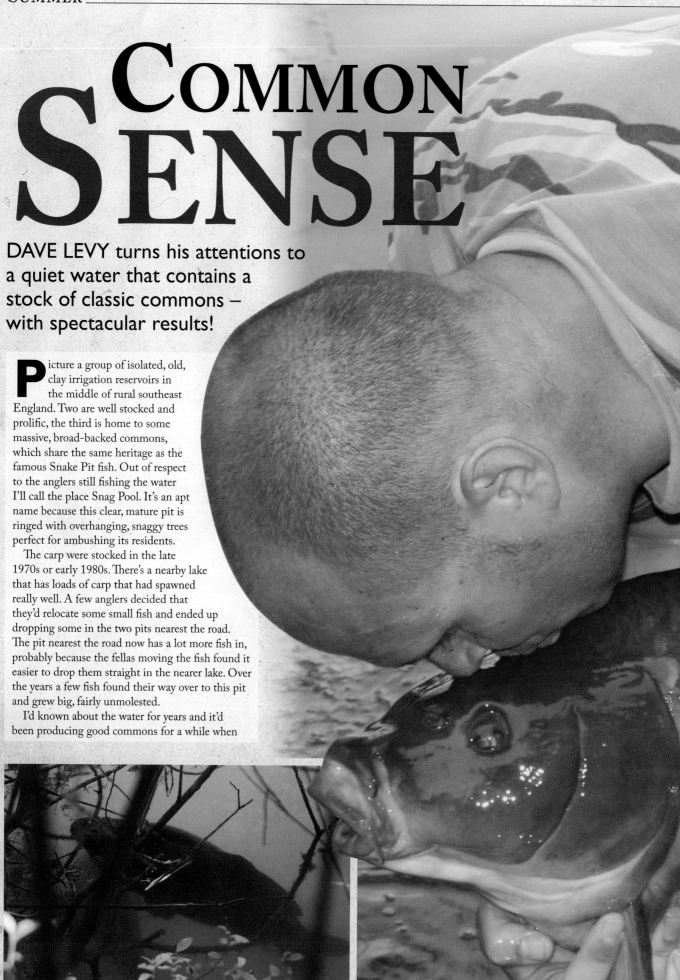

# COMMON SENSE

**DAVE LEVY turns his attentions to a quiet water that contains a stock of classic commons – with spectacular results!**

Picture a group of isolated, old, clay irrigation reservoirs in the middle of rural southeast England. Two are well stocked and prolific, the third is home to some massive, broad-backed commons, which share the same heritage as the famous Snake Pit fish. Out of respect to the anglers still fishing the water I'll call the place Snag Pool. It's an apt name because this clear, mature pit is ringed with overhanging, snaggy trees perfect for ambushing its residents.

The carp were stocked in the late 1970s or early 1980s. There's a nearby lake that has loads of carp that had spawned really well. A few anglers decided that they'd relocate some small fish and ended up dropping some in the two pits nearest the road. The pit nearest the road now has a lot more fish in, probably because the fellas moving the fish found it easier to drop them straight in the nearer lake. Over the years a few fish found their way over to this pit and grew big, fairly unmolested.

I'd known about the water for years and it'd been producing good commons for a while when

The carp were where they should have been – under the snags!

Pushing the baited rig close to the snaggy bushes was advantageous.

The massive common picked the bait up just to the left of this swim.

How many carpers carry one of these?

Leaning into a margin-hooked carp.

it threw up a spawnbound common of over 40lb. I didn't go down for a look back then because I figured that the fish would spawn out, and it duly did, coming out again at 35lb. Years later, when Neil Messenger had the big 'un at over 46lb, I realised that I had to get my act together because I was travelling a long way to fish the Brook and I now had huge fish on the doorstep.

The five to six-acre lake is day-only fishing and sees its fair share of anglers targeting the teeming masses of tench that live there. The main sub-surface feature is a central gravel bar, which shelves up on one side of the lake.

I'd been doing a few sessions during winter and I'd noted two really dense, uninterrupted areas of trees on the far bank. I thought that the fish would get well in there in summer. That area reminded me of CEMEX Sutton when I first fished there – during June, July and August the fish were always under the bushes. I didn't think that the fish here would be any different, and so it proved.

Carp are creatures of habit and they're all the same beast, just in different lakes.

During my winter sessions I came to the conclusion that if Two Tone came out of the Brook then I'd head down here. When Two Tone came out in June, sure enough, I was down at Snag Pool the next day. I saw a fish in the margins straightaway and baited a couple of shallower weedy spots with some Nash Hi Betaine Pellets and the new Bling bait. When I returned a week later, I found that the areas had been totally cleared. After baiting a few more times I noticed that the fish would feed on an area once, leave and not return. I was, therefore, looking for new opportunities for baiting and fishing each time I visited

– trying to set and spring new traps each session.

My first visit with the rods was eventful. I found a group of three fish in a corner with big snag bushes to the left and right. All three were good thirties, with the biggest looking like a comfortable upper thirty. They were going to and from the bushes, following each other, looking a bit spawny. I waited for half an hour for the fish to move out but they showed no signs of leaving. I decided that I'd try and semi-spook them from the area by sprinkling pellets on their heads. The shower of tiny morsels raining down over their impressive shoulders did nothing to shift them, so I decided to take the plunge and lower my rig straight in among the carp. I attached a PVA bag, crossed my fingers and dropped in. Shortly after placing the bag all three fish were tails up, right over it. I started to think that there was something wrong with my rig because the fish were still feeding hard over just one bag of pellets after 20 minutes. Just as I was getting really twitchy, the tip absolutely wrenched round to the left and whatever was attached ploughed through the snag bush like a steam train and carried on out the other side! I eased off a bit and let the fish go out – my line was pointing at the bush and the fish was probably 20 yards out in the lake. I had 20lb Bullet Braid on so I wasn't too worried about pulling the fish back to the bush

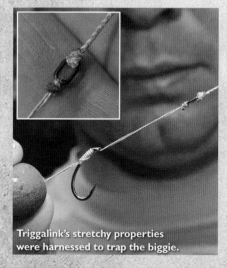

Triggalink's stretchy properties were harnessed to trap the biggie.

Bling and Hi Betaine pellets – the killer combination.

picked the hook bait up and dropped it. It left me a bit bemused as to why I hadn't hooked it, though. I decided on a bit of a rig change, swapping to Triggalink and lengthening the link. I set the link up as a combi-link joining the Triggalink to Ultrasilk braid with a small steel ring. The fish that had picked the hook bait up had drifted off so I decided to move.

I moved around to a spot in which I'd seen a few fish show. The heavens absolutely opened for about an hour and a half and, once it had abated, the lake went completely still and silent – I could see every bubble and bow wave as the fish went about their business.

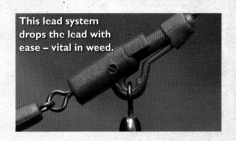

This lead system drops the lead with ease – vital in weed.

results fishing onto such areas in the past. As I write now, after the event, the area has cleared up and the clear spot is probably to size of half a bivvy. I started getting a load of liners in there when the weed was up but I think that they've lost a little confidence since the area has cleared up a bit.

## THE TWO BIG FISH, NOW JOINED BY ANOTHER ONE, CAME SWIMMING OUT FROM THE BUSH.

It appeared that the bulk of the carp were down at the opposite end of the lake so I grabbed my kit and headed over. I noticed a couple of big commons under the bushes to one side of the swim; one was probably a mid-thirty and the other was the big 'un. I wanted to get the spot baited and my rig into position as quietly as possible, so I decided to use a pole with a bait cup on the end to deliver the whole lot to its position on the end of the marginal bush.

The overhanging snag trees either side of the swim were a mixture of willows and alders which, at some points, overhung the swim by 10 or 15 feet. Dense beds of Canadian pondweed grow up to the edge of the tree line. I was dropping my bait onto a mixture of silkweed and Canadian, so not exactly clear, but I'm not worried about fishing into weed because I've had good

Anyway, I poled out my hook bait and one cupful of pellets nice and quietly. As I swung the pole back behind me the two big fish, now joined by another one, came swimming out from the bush. They circled the bait in about four feet of water just as the braid was settling. I was still standing there over my rod when the fish tailed up over the bait, I couldn't believe that I'd got away with it or that they dropped and fed so quickly. I didn't really want to move, so I just sat down by my rod as the braid twitched away in the clear water. It's a strange feeling, sitting there willing a mid-thirty common to avoid my bait as there was a bigger one feeding alongside it! I could see the two

Built for fighting! Dave scores with this 32lb belter.

and slowly started to retrieve line. As it approached the outer branches, swirling heavily on the surface, the carp shook its head and my tackle pinged clear of the bush! After that, it simply plodded up and down the margins a couple of times before I slipped it into the net.

It was a fish that I'd seen a photo of a year previously at 34lb 8oz. When I hoisted it onto the scales it registered 32lb, so the fish had obviously had a bit of a spawn. The first thing that I noticed was the condition of the fish; it was absolutely immaculate and its mouth was pristine – they don't get caught an awful lot in Snag Pool.

There was nobody else about so I had to do a self-take shot, which, fortunately, came out well. I put some bait back out in the snaggy corner but, after checking it a couple of times, it remained barren – even the tench that had been coming in and out had ghosted away.

I managed to pop down after work one night on a baiting run and noticed that the fish seemed to be using a couple of sets of snaggy trees on the far bank. I'd been sitting at work shortly after baiting and thought that if I went down there I'd get a fish. I found a couple of fish straightaway and managed to present a bait to them. I was able to watch a thirty approach my hook bait, pick it up and drop it immediately before moving off a few inches and continuing to feed. It didn't seem at all put off that it had

A cracking, 25lb common – live for the camera.

They don't get caught much in Snag Pool.

tails sticking out of the water as clear as day; the third fish seemed reluctant to feed – it was coming in and out of the swim without really getting its head down. It soon got to the point where I couldn't see anything of the fish apart from their tails; the water was so cloudy.

All of a sudden the big 'un rose off the bottom and shook its head two or three times – I'd hooked it! I still didn't have an alarm on so I stood up, as I did so the fish saw me and bolted, at which point my Baitrunner screamed! I grabbed the rod as the fish powered out into open water, not even flirting

with the snaggy trees either side of me! The fish ran for probably 20 yards and went down, deep, into 15 feet of water. It held its ground out in the main lake for a minute or so before making a lunge for the marginal weed. I crammed the pressure on because I really didn't want the fish to bog down in the weed. I could see it twisting in the clear margins as it tried to make sanctuary in the green stuff. As it rolled among the weed I was left in no doubt as to the fact that I had a 40lb common on and the old knees started to go! I stepped off the shelf expecting it to be waist deep, so I was surprised when I plunged into chest-deep water! Luckily the fish went straight into the net, as I'm not sure if I could have taken any more! On the scales it went 44lb 9oz, which was a bit weird because the day before I'd

been boxing stuff up to move house and had come across an old book that had a picture of Dick Walker with Clarissa at 44lb in it. I actually thought to myself: "God, I'd like to catch that now," and the next day there I was holding one of that size. The fish came from a lake that was notably hard and was absolutely mint, which made it even more special. I don't think that I've ever caught a fish that is so wild and powerful. When I was weighing it, it was flapping in the sling, virtually doing somersaults. It's just a really superbly proportioned carp – when I saw the picture of Neil Messenger with the fish I was blown away by it and it's partly the reason that I targeted it in the first place. I think that it's a fish that will simply get bigger and bigger. I'm not finished just yet on Snag Pool, I've bagged a 25-pounder since and I'd love to catch a few more of its stock, perhaps even the other big 'un that came out recently at 43lb!

Carp care is of paramount importance.

What a fish! 44lb 9oz of pristine English common.

# EARLY MORNING ASSAULT

If you're struggling for a bite there are ways to get a bend in the rod, as CHRIS ROSE and STEVE SPURGEON prove with a change of tactics on an early hours summer trip.

The gruesome twosome, Chris Rose and Steve Spurgeon, set their sights on Oxlease Lake on the Linear Fisheries complex in Oxford. As it's one of the busiest day ticket lakes in the country they're going to be up against it, but the rewards are certainly there to be had.

As the banks are usually heaving with eager carp anglers and finding two vacant swims side by side is rare on weekends.

Arriving at 6pm on a Friday we're stood in one of the reserved swims along the far bank with a vicious wind blowing straight into our faces.

"Hmm," starts Chris. "I don't fancy this. Steve and I only have light rods with us because we're waiting for some more powerful ones to be sent from Fox. With this wind and our soft rods we'll only be able to cast about 40 yards. Ideally we want to be fishing the middle, which is 100 to 110 yards out, so I reckon we should head to the opposite bank."

Maybe it's due to the poor weather forecast or the fact that it's FA Cup Final weekend, but there are a couple of free swims, two of which are directly opposite.

"They'll do," says Steve and they head straight for the empty swims.

Set up in the two swims, Chris and Steve have a quick thrash about with a marker rod. There's little difference in the lake bed on Oxlease, with the majority of the lake being clear and the occasional bit of gravel. Even so, Steve finds a seam of rough gravel at about 90 yards and Chris settles for a soft patch at 110 yards. With the light fading rapidly the two areas are treated to a dozen spodfuls of bait before the lads turn in for the night.

Come daylight, which is about 5am at this time of year, nothing's happened. No carp have been heard crashing out, no bite alarms have sounded and neither Chris nor Steve has received so much as a bleep. Not that the lads are worried of course, there's still plenty of time.

Steve starts out with zig rigs...

...and a sloppy spod mix over the top.

"If you observe the anglers on this lake, the majority of them are fishing at between 30 and 50 yards," says Chris. "While the lake is very busy this leaves a channel down the centre that's relatively free of lines and therefore relatively 'safe' for the carp. This is why we've both decided to fish the middle."

By 8am Steve's manning his spod rod once again.

"Last night I put out groundbait slop," says Steve as he launches his spod across the lake. "There was little food in the mix but loads of attraction. I've now topped up this slop with food particles. Broken boilies, corn, hemp and pellets have all been added so that I can get a bed of bait out there for the carp to get their heads down on."

With no indications forthcoming Chris opts for a change. Winding up his marker rod he fires it out across the water. After a few sweeps through the swim he pops the float up at 90 yards. He's found a small area of gravel with soft lake bed behind it.

"All of my rods were fishing over a soft bottom last night," explains Chris. "This new area will allow me to put one rod on the gravel, one on the edge of the gravel and one in the soft stuff, giving me more options and a better chance."

The rest of the morning passes with no signs of carp whatsoever. Both are surprised that they haven't had any liners because they are using braided main line.

"Using tight, braided main lines, although there's a slight drop on the indicators, will give us excellent bite indication," explains Steve. "It will pick up any movement on the line, including fish bumping into it. The distinct lack of indications leads me to believe that there are no carp in front of us at this particular moment. If I were getting liners but no bites then it would mean that there were fish in the swim but my presentation was wrong and a new rig or bait would be in order."

## CHRIS ROSE'S DAY TICKET TACTICS

**1** You'll need some soft expander pellets and PVA stocking.

**2** Pour around 30 or so of the pellets into the PVA.

**3** Compress the pellets into the end of the PVA tube.

**4** Use the plunger to push the pellets through, letting out PVA as you do so.

**5** Tie the PVA off nice and tightly to form a small stick, like this one.

**6** Thread it onto the hook link, but be sure to keep the hook point clear, as shown.

"For this session I've employed a few little tactics to try and gain an edge. I'm whittling my hook baits down to alter their shape and soaking them in dip. Not only does this boost their attraction but it hardens them too. I've also camouflaged my leadcore leaders with a black marker pen because, looking at the margins, the lake bed is very dark."

As the afternoon wears on the wind turns, blowing straight up the lake. It starts drizzling and the sky clouds over. Chris is hopeful that this sudden change in conditions will turn the carp onto the feed. He explains that even a subtle change in conditions can often be the trigger needed to kick-start a lake into action.

In waters such as Oxlease, where there's a huge head of carp, it will only take a few fish to start feeding to trigger the others, such is the competitive nature of the fish in well-stocked venues.

Just to confirm his thoughts the guy set up next to Chris promptly banks a 15lb mirror, shortly followed by a guy

**Steve gives a display of accurate spodding...**

**Rods out, it's time to wait for a bite.**

**... and Chris recasts in search of carp.**

Chris lends a helping hand.

The duo are well pleased as their efforts pay off.

on the opposite bank banking a smaller carp. Rather than the whole lake kicking into action things swing in the opposite direction and, as quickly as those two bites came, the lake completely dies once more. Nevertheless, Chris continues to trickle bait in, dropping a couple of spods over his baits every hour or so.

Concerned that all is not going exactly as they wanted the lads come up with a contingency plan.

"Although a lake is fishing poorly it can often be the case that another lake nearby can be producing," says Chris. "Luckily, Linear Fisheries has a number of well-stocked waters that we can try if carp are being caught."

## OCCASIONALLY A SMALL BLACK SHAPE MIGHT APPEAR AS A BACK BREAKS THE SURFACE.

"We'll check Brasenose One and Two and if either of these are fishing well we'll move," continues Steve. "As our car is locked in the car park until the gates open at 9am tomorrow, I'll pack up at 4am and leave most of my kit with Chris. I'll take my rods, alarms and a few bits and pieces and I'll head over to Brasenose. Chris will join me once the gates are unlocked."

It seems that most people fishing Brasenose One have caught and, seeing that a couple of anglers are stood playing fish, it looks as if this lake will offer a better chance. As luck would have it there's a free swim on the far bank, which will hopefully remain empty until morning. However, the rest of the lake is packed, but it doesn't seem to have affected the carp too much.

At four o'clock the following morning Steve packs his gear away. Putting three rods, alarms, a bait bucket and suchlike into the back of the car, Steve sets off towards Brasenose One.

By 4.50am Steve is firmly ensconced in the free swim on the far bank. With everyone else still in their bivvies he launches three rigs into open water, just 10 yards apart, and puts 15 spodfuls of bait over the area.

Sat looking across the water we see three carp crash, all in different areas, but that's more than has been seen on Oxlease in the past 30 hours or so. An alarm shatters the silence as someone at the end of the lake is in. Over the next hour and a half six carp are landed, but none have come to Steve's rods. There's a quick call to Chris to tell of his woes and things become worse.

"There are carp crashing all over your baited area," says Chris. "I've repositioned

A chunky mirror falls to Steve's zig.

one of my rods among them, but I've had nothing as yet."

By 8am the temperature's soaring and more and more movement can be seen on the surface.

"If you watch the water closely when it's calm you'll see small ripples and creases caused by carp moving just below the surface," says Steve. "Occasionally a small black shape might appear as a back breaks the surface, again giving away a carp's presence. Recognising these subtle signs allows you to target the carp before other less observant anglers and therefore you can reap the rewards.

"It does look like there's a lot of carp movement near the surface, so I reckon a change of tactics is on the cards."

Having had no action on the bottom Steve ties up two zig rigs. The water in front of him is roughly 10 feet deep, so Steve ties one 6ft zig and one 9ft zig. Using zigs at different depths allows you to cover more water as one depth will invariably be more productive than others. Once you start catching, change all of your rigs to the same depth as the productive one to capitalise on the action.

With two zigs out in the lake Steve adds a bit of water to his spod mix, making it sloppy so that it will create a cloud in the water. This is then spodded over the top of the zigs and the results are almost instant. The 6ft zig proves its worth because the bobbin drops to the floor and Steve's in – at last. Playing it quite hard, to

The biggest fish to Chris' rods goes just over 18lb.

**1** A trimmed boilie with a plastic sweetcorn hair stop is the hook bait.

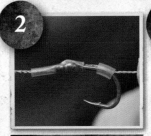
**2** The rig features a short-shanked hook and some shrink tubing, as shown.

**3** A Fox Kwik Change Clip makes switching rigs easy. I use them all the time.

**4** A simple lead-clip system is still Steve's first choice on most waters.

**5** A 3ft leadcore leader behind the lead keeps everything pinned down on the deck.

**6** He breaks up the leadcore's lines by using a marker pen to mottle it.

keep the fish from fouling the other lines, a little mirror of about 8lb is soon in the net.

With the carp returned Steve casts the rig, complete with the same bait that he's just caught on, back out.

"When action really gets going you can often catch a number of carp on the same hook bait," explains Steve. "It allows you to spend more time fishing and therefore more time catching carp. It's something that Chris and I started doing in the British Carp Angling Championship matches, when time is particularly precious, and it has worked on many an occasion since."

Two more spodfuls of slop are put over the area before Steve's in again. This fish is similar to the first, although it just makes double figures.

With two bites on the 6ft zig and none on the 9ft, Steve reels in the longer zig, chops it down to six feet and recasts. The rig has barely had time to settle when it's away again.

"If you can really get them going on this tactic then it's crazy," Steve explains. "Double takes are not uncommon."

As the third carp of the morning slides over the net cord Chris turns up in the swim. Having packed all of the kit away into his car he is armed with just a single rod.

Winding in the bottom bait, leaving Steve's two zigs out there, Chris casts his rod, complete with a 6ft hooklength and a small pop-up, to the spot. Placing it on the alarm the pair of them get to work spodding slop over the rigs.

Steve's in once again and promptly lands another smallish mirror. Before he's got time to unhook it his other rod screams off. Leaving Chris to unhook and return the carp, Steve bends into a Brasenose One fish for the fourth time that morning. Chris gets ready to net Steve's carp but drops the net and picks up his rod. With both Chris and Steve playing carp it's hard to believe the frantic action after so many eventless hours on Oxlease. The only rod left without a carp attached to it bursts into action, it really is crazy.

Steve slips the net under a lovely looking 15lb 10oz mirror while Chris' fish turns out to be slightly bigger and tips the scales at just over 18lb.

With the third carp safely in the net we set about taking a few pictures before packing up. Chris has to get back to Essex by noon and, with it being past 10am already, he's in somewhat of a rush.

After such a desperate struggle on Oxlease it's hard to believe that the final two hours of the session have produced seven carp.

This just goes to prove that if you are prepared to adapt, the rewards are there for the taking.

**Once the tactics come right, the lads help themselves to loads of these.**

Back you go, little fella. Fetch your mum and dad!

The world of design and technology never ceases to amaze. Just when you think "how can this get any better?" the next generation comes along and leaves you awe-struck. At Daiwa we are constantly at the cutting edge of design and development, which is why we consistently offer you awesome, ground breaking tackle. So let us introduce you to our next generation of Tournament® Basia 'big pit' reels - the **Tournament® Basiair**. The lightness of this powerhouse is hard to believe, weighing in at only 445 grams! But don't let this fool you, it's as tough and smooth as any of its illustrious predecessors. The Basiair's lightness is achieved using a combination of 'AirMetal' magnesium alloy and ultra light ZAION, combined to push the boundaries of reel design. Still retaining a massive line retrieval of just under 90cm per handle turn, the 'free spool' function of QD plus a super compact construction, the Basiar takes carping to a new level of genius.

The world's biggest specialist.

# A Basiair of pure genius

# CLOSE ENCOUNTERS

The margins are one of the best features on any water, as DAVE MAGALHAES proves by bagging the biggest carp in his lake on a midsummer trip.

Use a spod to drop bait onto margin spots accurately.

Returning another carp from the margin from whence it came!

Dave carefully weighs a 30lb-plus carp.

A good 80 per cent of my fishing is done in the margins, and even my surface fishing is done quite close in. When the carp are in the edge I can see them and watch what they're up to and react to it, giving me the best chance of catching one.

When I started fishing, most anglers would sling their rigs out and wait for the alarm to scream. I'd sit there and occasionally see a fish moving close to the bank. Eventually, I started to creep to the water's edge and investigate the movement and would sometimes find fish feeding extremely close in – that was it, I was hooked. Finding the fish and watching them is so much more exciting than sitting behind motionless rods.

Tipping the scales at 33lb...

Working for a living, as most of us do, I can only go fishing on my day off, or for a quick overnight session. Sitting behind my rods drives me mad because I think that I'm wasting time. I'd much rather be baiting spots, finding the carp and watching them than simply sitting there waiting. At least when I'm watching them, even if I don't catch them, I feel like I've done something productive because I'm learning about their behaviour. This is especially true of the bigger carp that I target because they all have their own characters. The more you watch them, the more you pick up on certain habits, all of which can be used towards catching them.

On the park lake that I'm fishing today I know that the biggest carp in here loves boilies and spends a lot of its time around the island. I put loads of boilies around the island when I arrived, put a rod on the spot and shortly after landed that carp at 33lb. I'm not saying that everything goes quite as smoothly as that all the time, but knowing the fish that you're after will help you catch it. In fact, this carp was my first thirty, which I caught when I was 19, and I caught it a few years later too – so it's nice to see him again. On a different water that I'm going to target I know roughly when the target fish is due to be caught and I know that it loves to eat particles. Information like this allows me to make the absolute most of my time and it all stems from finding the fish in the edge.

My carp fishing started off on park lakes and this is where I first realised the benefits of fishing in the edge, but I really got my teeth into it when I moved onto larger gravel pits where the water was crystal clear. There was one pit in particular where a lot of the regulars were fishing out in the middle of the lake at about 200 yards. Everyone that I spoke to said that the middle is where you want to be fishing, and to be fair they were catching. However, I was walking around the lake and finding carp that they'd never seen, getting right in under my feet. I found a group of six commons, all of which were 30lb plus, and I managed to keep them there all day by dropping some bait in the edge and getting up a nearby tree to watch them

come in and clear up every last morsel before they drifted out into open water. I'd drop a little more bait in and they'd come straight back in and start feeding and I simply kept repeating the process. Ever since then I have never been able to sit behind motionless rods. If the going tactic is to fish out in the lake then it's a fair bet that the carp will move into the margins to get away from the pressure. When everyone is fishing to the middle of the lake, but there's not much being caught, it's a dead giveaway that the carp are getting in the edge. After all, if the middle of the lake is so good, why isn't everybody catching?

Every lake lends itself to a margin approach because carp simply love to get

... One Peck is a great reward for Dave's stalking efforts.

in the edge. That said, your job is made simpler on clear lakes where you can find the carp easily, and it helps if it's quiet too. If you're fishing a lake where the water's murky you can still find the fish by looking for water movement, caused by carp moving under the surface. Bow waves and creases on the surface are a sure sign of fish movement and easy to spot once you know what you're looking for. The more you look, the better you'll become at spotting the signs.

as comfortable being in the edge as they are further out in the lake, so you can spook them easier. Once you have, they probably won't return for a good few hours, so be careful.

This also goes for keeping noise to a minimum. It's quite surprising how loud you can be without realising it, so be aware of the noise that you're making. Setting up back from the water's edge will help with this and it'll also keep you out of sight. What's more, don't have

My margin rig, ready to be placed in the edge.

## THE CARP LOVE TO GET IN CLOSE ALONG THE WINDWARD BANK ON A NEW WIND.

Most anglers will look at an island and want to fish close to it because it's the main feature, but surely the margin is the biggest feature on any lake. It's a natural food trap as well, because food falls into the lake, drops off trees and bushes and gets thrown in by anglers. Hot, sunny days are great for finding carp in the margins, generally due to the margins being quite shallow. Also, the carp love to get in close along the windward bank on a new wind, especially a warm southwesterly in summer. If you are going to fish the margins on a sunny day then pay attention to where your shadow is being cast. You can be walking along the bank and your shadow passes over the carp because you haven't spotted them. All you'll see is the bow wave as they bolt out into the lake. Carp aren't

your rods sticking out over the water, only have the tip ring protruding from the bank where possible. Keep your line concealed by fishing with slack lines. I use leadcore leaders too, but I don't use back leads because I don't like them bouncing around on my line while I'm playing a fish.

Although the margins are brilliant areas to target, there are times when they're less productive. As a general rule, I'd give it a miss from November through to the end of February. During the coldest months the carp tend to move out in the lake and hang semi-dormant mid-water. As soon as we get the first sunny, spring days the carp will move in and look for food.

When it comes to targeting carp close in I will walk circuits of the lake and

check all the likely spots until I find them. Only then will I set about trying to catch one. As well as looking for the carp, I look for areas where they have been. Clean spots on the lake bed are usually down to feeding activity and areas of cloudy/coloured water are a dead giveaway. Be aware that you could be looking for really subtle signs, so don't amble into a swim expecting the carp to be blatantly obvious. Where you get undercut banks the carp can be sitting under your feet and the only sign might be a tail poking out. I don't set traps and wait for the carp to find them. As I said earlier, time is precious; so when I'm fishing I want to be on fish.

## THE PERFECT MARGIN SET-UP

**1**

Splice a small loop in both ends of a metre-long leadcore leader.

**2**

Thread the leader through the small end of a ring swivel.

**3**

Pass one end of the leader through the loop in the opposite end.

**4**

Pull the leader down tight to secure the ring swivel at one end, like this.

**5**

Thread a tail rubber onto the leader so that the thick end faces the swivel.

**6**

Push the swivel into the end of an inline lead. I favour the Atomic Tackle Dung Bombs.

**7**

The swivel should sit like this. Note how the leader runs over the lead.

**8**

Push the tail rubber onto the lead, trapping the leader in place.

The margin tactics come good, as they have many times before.

Boilies are my favourite hook bait.

When you find carp in the edge do not simply drop your rig among them and expect to catch one. I wait for them to move off and then carefully lower a rig into position and wait for them to return, which they invariable do. Dropping the rig will cause the lead to thump on the lake bed and this can spook the fish. If they won't move then you can 'irritate' them by carefully flicking tiny baits at them. I'm talking about three or four 2mm or 3mm pellets at most, not a handful of boilies. Generally, the fish will move for long enough for you to get a rig in place. If the carp are browsing and not settling in one area then I will find a clear spot just up the bank and wait for them to move onto it. One thing that I've noticed over the years is that big beds of bait in the edge spook them more often than not, so only put a handful in at a time. Remember, you are only fishing for one bite at a time; you are not trying to hold the carp in one area for your entire session.

Boilies are by far my favourite hook bait, and that doesn't just apply to fishing in the margins. Maggots are fantastic for feeding and make a huge difference, but I don't like using them on soft lake beds because I think they bury themselves out of sight. A mixture of particles and crushed boilies is generally what I feed because I like to use a mixture of bits. Having a mixture of baits helps to confuse them and makes them easier to catch.

I've caught most of my big carp from the margins. In fact, my PB of 49lb 10oz came just three and a half feet from the bank but, to be fair, most of my time is spent margin fishing so I'm bound to catch most of my fish close in. It's definitely an area worth targeting and you'll learn loads even if you're not catching, so give it a try.

A fiesty ghost common caught just two feet from the bank.

# FLOATER FISHING MADE EASY!

JIM SHELLEY thinks that people make floater fishing harder than it needs to be. Join him at CEMEX Horton to see how easy it can be...

A lot of people seem to find floater fishing difficult. In this article I'll show you how to make it easy. People make it harder for themselves when, in fact, it should be easier each time that you get the floater rod out.

I've done a lot of my floater fishing on CEMEX Horton Church Lake in recent years. Many of the big fish in here tend to fall to surface baits once or twice each year, sometimes even more. When you get these Horton fish going on the surface in front of you it's an awesome sight. We're talking about a water that contains between 70 and 80 fish, which, at the right time of year, includes sixty 30lb-plus fish, so it's exciting fishing. I've had a little glimpse of how swiftly you can get fish going and just how quick you have to be to take advantage.

For too many people, floater fishing is a quick affair for the wrong reasons. If they get blown out early on you can literally see their morale seeping away. A lot of would-be floater anglers have problems with the techniques involved and end up criticising those that do catch carp off the top. Some anglers go to great lengths to demean floater captures, proclaiming that they 'don't count' or that surface fishing is 'cheating'.

## I FIND THAT FISH COME TO ASSOCIATE THE CRASH OF THE SPOD WITH FOOD.

The first thing that anglers tend to struggle with is actually getting their freebies into areas in which the carp feel secure enough to accept them. You can catapult free offerings, or PVA bag them but, to be honest, I favour the spod. It might not seem like the subtlest tool for floater fishing but on waters such as Horton I find that the fish come to associate the crash of the spod with food – it's like a dinner gong to them. Over the past three years the fish on here have really got into their floating food and, like I said, it's an awesome sight when they get going.

During these three years the fishing has become a lot harder but I've got a few tricks up my sleeve to keep them coming. First up is the new controller

Horton carp taking floaters from Jim's oil-slicked area.

PURE CRUSTACEAN EXTRACT
EEE'S ESSENTIAL EXTRACTS
APPROX 250ml

NASH BAIT

PROVEN BAITS THAT MY MATES AND I ALWAYS USE. FISH WELL AND I GUARANTEE YOU WILL HAVE A RESULT! Kevin Nash

The awesome Crustacean Extract – it draws the fish to Jim.

Pimple, a Longfield original, falls victim to Jim's surface tactics.

from Nash. I used to use the more conventional Drennan teardrop-style controller, with the weight in the bottom. I went through a period of two sessions where I bumped off about 15 fish until Beadle showed me one of the TFG inline controllers. The first bite I had resulted in a 30lb fish and I was converted.

Moving on to more recent times, Kevin Nash sent me a sample of controllers that he'd been working on. These were similar to the TFG ones, although the Nash versions were heavier and had a concave end to increase the resistance to taking fish – making them more likely to bolt. The only drawback was that they weren't very aerodynamic and didn't fly much more than 40 yards. After using the samples I went back to Gary Bayes at Nash and told him not to worry about the concave feature and simply make a heavier version of the TFG controller.

I now have two controllers, one 3oz and one 5oz. I must admit that I'm saving the 5oz version for when the going gets really tough. These things are mega, I can now hit 120 yards comfortably with the 3oz version and 10lb main line.

## AS SOON AS THE FISH SHOW SIGNS OF FEEDING GET YOUR RIG IN THERE.

I don't use a special floater rod for my surface fishing, I go for the 12ft 3.5lb test curve Nash Pursuits, which allow me to throw these heavy controllers a long way. Due to their weight, drift doesn't affect these quite as much as conventional controllers; they just sit out there. Because they are so weighty the fish tend to hook themselves. This means that I can fish two rods, flick the free spools on and wait for them to rattle off.

There isn't anything complicated about my hooking arrangement either. My hook link of choice is olive, satin Drennan Double Strength in 10lb tied direct to a size 10 hook. I don't drop below 10lb hook links – I'm not messing about; once I've hooked the fish I want to get it in. You won't see me using any bands or loops; I just go for a longish nylon hair. My hook baits are fluorescent orange pop-ups that I make

What a beast – 38lb 8oz of CEMEX Kingsmead No1 mirror.

A pristine 28lb Horton common with a taste for floaters.

myself. I put one of these on one rod and play around with different coloured baits, double baits, treble baits and the like on the other.

The carp don't really like to feed in the wind on Horton, so I create my own flat spots. I use the Nash Bait Strawberry Oil Palatant and CC Moore hemp oil as well as the awesome Nash Crustacean Oil. I've noticed that even when it's calm I can actually pull fish to me with the Crustacean Oil. All you need to do is pour it onto your floaters in a bag. I use the large CC Moore Trout Pellet Floaters, and ensure that they are well coated.

When I floater fish I really do go for it. Yesterday, I was eight hours into my session getting tunnel vision and becoming dehydrated. I was receiving

**Jim leans into an explosive surface-snared carp!**

these inspections and explosions as the fish veered away at the last moment, yet the answer was staring me in the face. My hook link became caught in a tree and when I pulled it down there was a knot in it, which had shortened its length. I thought: "You plank, there's the answer." I shortened my link down to two and a half feet and had a 30lb 4oz mirror first chuck!

I had fish feeding more or less as soon as I put the floaters out today. You really have to be on the ball here because the feeding can stop as soon as it starts. I've managed to bag a PB 38lb-plus grassie and I pulled out of another fish. Don't waste time feeding the carp, trickling the mixers in; as soon as the fish show signs of feeding get your rig in there. You're there to catch them not to feed them!

The massive hits that I've been having on the floaters have made it clear to me that, rather than wasting my time sitting behind static rods, waiting for small windows of opportunity, it is better to get at them with the floaters. It's all part of learning about our sport – we all want to catch a carp so you might as well have a go. This is an easy way to catch carp from the surface, you don't need to time the strike, you don't need to take much stuff with you, just loads of floaters and a spod rod plus a few of these controllers. I can assure you that you will catch carp off the top like this.

Jaws at 28lb. No carp is safe in the water with Jim around.

I'll bring you up to date with the catches that I've had off the top. The opening on Horton was incredible – even by Horton's ridiculously high standards. There were something like 20 thirties out. I knew that it was busy down there so I left it until the next week.

Nobody had really been giving the floater fishing much of a crack. I got down and was straight on the fish. My first fish off the top was Jaws, a mirror, at 28lb. The next day I managed to get some fish going in The Sick swim. They were taking quite close in so I whacked the controller out a long way before

Jim keeps his surface hook links tidy in a plastic bag – ready for action.

Jim's home-made floater hook baits are pukka...

... but he rates these ready-rolled ones as well.

These floats have changed Jim's surface fishing for good.

Time for one last picture before Scar – 40lb 4oz of prime Horton mirror – is returned safely.

drawing it back over the feeding carp. I put the rod onto the ground and sat down. After a short while I noticed that a fish had taken the bait into its mouth without bolting. I struck into the fish and it set off on an 80-yard run down the left-hand margin. There are quite a few bushes along that margin and I had lost fish in the past when they'd done this so I was a little worried. Fortunately, following some toing and froing, I managed to get the fish back and slip it into the net. It was Scar, a fish that I'd caught at 37lb plus last year. This time it weighed in at an impressive 40lb 4oz, another new forty for Horton and my third surface-caught forty.

I moved lakes the following day, heading over to the Road Lake where I managed to trip up a 30lb 2oz mirror and lost an absolute beast that arced across the lake and into a set of snags.

On the third day of my floater fishing session I signed into Horton again. As I walked onto the lake I saw a few fish feeding on some floaters that had drifted down to the lodge end. I thought that it would be rude not to have a go. I was away almost immediately after casting in. I played the fish in and upon slipping the net under it I realised that it was an original Longfield carp named Pimple, a common of 35lb 2oz.

# SEEING CLEARLY

On venues with gin-clear water, carp can become extremely wary of even the most subtle presentations. DAVE ELLYATT reveals how to fool them using fluorocarbon.

During winter the clarity of our waters starts to improve significantly. Weed growth begins to die back and the heavy end tackle employed throughout summer becomes arguably more conspicuous during the daylight hours. It's now time for fluorocarbon to come into play.

Fluorocarbon is a clear monofilament that has three obvious advantages when used as a hook link or main line. It has the same light refractive index as water – when submerged this makes it virtually invisible. Its specific gravity makes it denser than water and ensures that hook links and main lines sink quickly and lie tight to the bottom. It is rather 'hard' compared to nylon monofilament, so is very abrasion resistant.

Fluorocarbon migrated into carp fishing from the fly fishing sector. Initially, it was treated with suspicion by many carp anglers, the main reason being that, in general, it lacked stretch and impact resistance. However, this has greatly improved and there are numerous fluorocarbons on the market that have all the right assets to make them a viable alternative for carp fishing.

It can be superb for use as a main line. Anybody that has used the more popular fluorocarbon main lines will tell you that they sink like a brick and are virtually invisible. I would say that these are the two main attributes that I look for in a main line and I would be willing to compromise relative strength.

In many angling situations these benefits can outweigh their disadvantages, in that they do not cast as well as nylon monofilament in the higher breaking strains, due to their inherent stiffness, and are, diameter for diameter, not very strong.

X-Line has become widely used over the last few years. For its diameter it is relatively weak but, unlike most fluorocarbons, what X-Line loses in strength seems to be largely compensated by its very stretchy nature, so impact resistance is improved.

I believe that fluorocarbon monofilament is highly underrated as a leader material. It can give the angler a major edge in some situations, yet very few people use it as a leader.

I first used it as a leader last year on Dinton Pastures near Reading, which is a notoriously weedy and fairly tricky water that is home to a good head of very big carp.

I can't remember exactly why I decided to use fluorocarbon as my leader material, rather than the usual leadcore, though. I think it was because I only had a two-

Fluorocarbon makes a great leader material. Put simply, the fish can't see it.

## THE LEADER KNOT

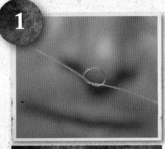

**1** Create a single overhand knot in your leader but don't pull down tight just yet.

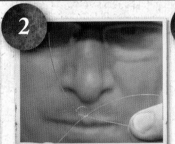

**2** Carefully poke the end of your main line through the small loop, like so.

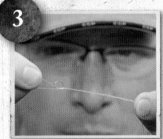

**3** Now wrap the main line over the leader 10 times and hold tight.

**4** Moisten the fluorocarbon with saliva. This will keep the tightening smooth.

**5** Now wrap the line back down the leader six times and go back through the loop.

**6** Keep your hands steady and slowly pull the knot tight. It should bed down neatly.

**7** The knot is extremely strong and will withstand large amounts of pressure.

**8** To finish off the knot, simply trim the tag ends carefully. Job done!

night guest session and I was determined to catch because there was unlikely to be a second chance in the near future. Therefore, I needed any edge and I felt that using fluorocarbon leaders rather than leadcore would set me apart from the majority of anglers on what is a fairly pressurised lake. I was using 5ft leaders connected to the main line using the 'carrot' leader knot (see photo sequence).

To cut a long story short, I managed to catch a 22lb 4oz mirror and a 26lb 10oz common. Out of the other 20 or so anglers on the lake that weekend, only one other caught. That was Alan Cooper who caught The Sandy Linear at 38lb odd and a smaller one.

The strange thing was that after I packed up and walked back to the car park, Alan was winding in one of his rods and I couldn't help but notice that he too was using clear leaders. Coincidence? Maybe, but it certainly gave me a lot of confidence in the fluoro leaders.

After that first trial I decided to increase the length of the leader to about 20 feet. This equates to four or five turns on the reel, plus the length of the rod and then about a 6ft drop for casting.

This results in a good length of heavy, invisible, abrasion-resistant material between the angler and the baited area, meaning that there is really very little for a line-shy carp to detect. One tip is to stretch out the leader as much as possible to remove the coiled memory from the spool.

I discussed the relative merits of fluorocarbon leaders with Leon Bartropp. He started using them in 20ft lengths last winter on Bellmere, a relatively tricky, clear water in the Colne Valley that he featured in his diary series in Advanced Carp Fishing. Leon initially used the fluorocarbon on just one rod, with leadcore leaders on the other two.

A lovely 20lb-plus mirror from a gin-clear estate lake.

Fast-sinking fluorocarbon can make a decent main line as well as a leader.

# THE FLUOROCARBON COMBI-RIG

**1** I always use ESP Ghost fluorocarbon; it's practically invisible in water.

**2** Cut off a length of around 15 inches. This will be enough to form the rig.

**3** Create a simple figure-of-eight loop at one end of the fluorocarbon, like so.

**4** Now take each end of the material between your thumb and forefinger.

**5** Twist the fluorocarbon by rolling your fingers in opposite directions.

**6** Twist up to two inches and then hold the spring section tightly between your fingers.

**7** Form another figure-of-eight loop in the material, creating a spring boom.

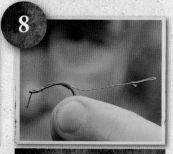

**8** Next, create a simple knotless knot using Dacron hooklength.

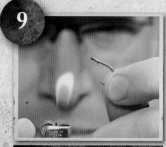

**9** Trim the Dacron near to the hook and then blob the remaining tag end.

**10** Your hooklength should now look neat and ready to be tied to the fluorocarbon.

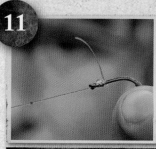

**11** Tie the fluorocarbon to the hook using the whipping knot (see sequence overleaf).

**12** Finally, attach your chosen hook baits. I use a boilie tipped with plastic corn.

# WANNA CATCH MORE CARP? OF COURSE YOU DO...

He began to receive bites on the rod with the fluorocarbon leader and its effectiveness became even more apparent when he fished leadcore and fluorocarbon side by side over the same spot. Surprise, surprise, all the bites came to the fluoro rod. Leon ended up fishing all three rods with fluoro leaders and his tally for the winter campaign was something like 10 30lb-plus carp, including a low forty, plus numerous smaller fish.

Many anglers struggle to tie the leader knot to attach the fluorocarbon to the main line but with practice it can be very easy.

The knot that I employ is usually called the surfcaster's knot or carrot knot because of its pointed, streamlined shape. Importantly, both tag ends point back up the line and the knot's tapered shape helps it fly through the rings.

Making the last section of line nearest the hook invisible is obviously a massive edge. It's unlikely to arouse suspicion from the carp and with the fluorocarbon's inherent stiffness it lends itself to anti-eject rigs.

As the sun's rays burn away the morning mist, I'm out of the bivvy playing a hard-fighting carp.

Use longer hairs with supple braid.

Fluorocarbon fools even the wariest of carp.

I started playing around with fluorocarbon hook links early last year. I was particularly impressed by its almost complete lack of visibility in water, its relative stiffness, the fact that it sank like a brick and was also relatively easy to straighten out under tension over a steaming kettle. I thought that it could be a significant edge on clear waters that had been hammered on coated braids and where the fish were becoming increasingly 'riggy' during daylight hours.

However, I wanted, if possible, to improve the stretch and impact resistance of a fluorocarbon hook link.

## THE WHIPPING KNOT

**1**
Push the line through the eye of your chosen hook pattern, like so.

**2**
Form a loop along the shank of the hook, keeping it open with a baiting needle.

**3**
Whip up the hook eight times, keeping it tight, and go back through the loop.

**4**
Moisten and slowly pull the knot tight. This will bed it down perfectly.

## THE PROOF

Knowing that all my end tackle is concealed, I await action.

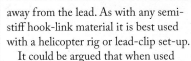

Rub the fluorocarbon over your knee to straighten.

Then I remembered the 'twizzled' Powergum boom used by match anglers when feeder fishing. This consists of a Powergum loop that is twisted to create a spring-like shock absorber. I could see the potential benefits of this system on fluorocarbon, so I tied a few up using 12lb Ghost and a size 9 Long-Shanx with a D on the shank of the hook that was extended with shrink tubing.

The shock-absorbing, spring-like boom at the swivel end significantly increases the stretch in the fluorocarbon compared to when it is tied on in the usual way. This greatly improves impact strength. The 'spring' section is obviously stiffer than the rest of the hook link and acts as a boom, helping to lay the link out away from the lead. As with any semi-stiff hook-link material it is best used with a helicopter rig or lead-clip set-up.

It could be argued that when used with a heavy, semi-fixed lead the rig's spring-like 'elastic' element will stretch when a carp pricks itself and help to pull the hook in deeper, making it more difficult to eject, in much the same way that Nash's Triggalink functions.

I tie the hook on using a 'Nigel Sharp' (NS) whipping knot rather than a knotless knot. This is because if you use a stiff hook-link material such as fluorocarbon on a hook with an inturned eye, the angle created by a knotless knot as the line exits the eye really closes the gape of the hook. This is because the line exits the eye coming from over the top of the knot 'barrel', whereas with the NS knot the line exits the eye from under the knot. I prefer the shallower angle that you get with the NS knot, which is still enough to make the hook turn on ejection, but not enough to close up the gape.

The fluorocarbon approach brings a stunningly scaled mirror in excess of 25lb.

# CUP-AND-DOWN CARPING

JAN PORTER demonstrates the almost-forgotten art of float legering, and shows how some spur of the moment floater fishing can catch carp like this...

Float legering is a craft that was, and still is, mainly adopted by 'general' coarse anglers targeting bream and tench, although it's rarely seen on the banks these days and seems to have been forgotten by many. I think it must be down to the trend that we carp anglers always seem to abide by – sitting there behind three rods placed on bite alarms seems to be the 'in' (and only) thing to do.

Well, by float legering with a little bit of thought and creation you can often catch just as many carp as the lazy anglers who wait for their alarms to sing. With this in mind, we join Jan Porter on the banks of Willow Pool, near Evesham, to learn the art of float legering.

Jan is located at the far end of the small but intimate pool, ready to cast out a funny-looking contraption. It consists of a rather large bubble float, an open-ended cage feeder and a double-boilie hook bait. He then casts the tackle into the margins and sprinkles a pouchful of casters over the top.

"I can't believe more anglers don't float fish for carp," Jan comments. "They're completely oblivious to the different line angles a float provides and you can definitely catch more carp as a result.

## HOW TO SET UP A FLOAT LEGER

**1** These are the components that you'll need to form the float leger.

**2** Attach a float stop onto your main line, by simply threading it on.

**3** Follow this with a buoyant, bubble-style pike float.

**4** Now thread on an open-ended cage feeder. This will hold groundbait.

**5** The feeder then needs to be pushed over a small, tapered rubber.

**6** Adjust the float stop to the required depth and you're ready to go!

"When you're fishing the typical carp set-up of semi-fixed leads, your line cuts through the water and stands out like a sore thumb. Carp will often become very wary of lines, and a different approach can catch them off guard. This is what float legering achieves.

"The main line stretches across the surface of the water and sits vertically below the bubble float, forming a completely different line angle. Carp can then approach the hook bait from 360

The float creates a permament marker for loose feed.

degrees without coming into contact with bowstring-tight lines. This will lower their guard and induce them into feeding confidently."

Jan tightens the main line and, with both rods cast at close quarters, places them onto the rod pod and keeps an eye on each float. The visible markers give him the opportunity to keep bait trickling over the top of the hook baits on a little-and-often basis. They're not there to indicate a bite; they just provide a different line angle and a marker to introduce freebies around.

The float leger should look like this!

Jan receives a twitch on the float.

"The other advantage of the float-legering style is the constant stream of food laying next to your hook bait," continues Jan. "I like to place a mixture of groundbait, casters and sweetcorn into the open-ended feeder. All carp love a caster because it's natural and anglers seem to have a mentality that believes only boilies catch carp. A different approach will often pay dividends, so give it a try!"

The gloomy sky then gives way to the odd break of sun, which begins to warm the water and bring the carp to the surface. Every now and then we notice a pair of lips slurp in the surface film then retreat back to the depths. The fish are obviously active, so a bite surely can't be far away.

## A BLACK SHAPE EMERGES FROM THE LILIES AND BOW WAVES ACROSS THE LAKES.

Sweetcorn's great on commercial waters.

The right-hand bobbin begins to twitch and rise as carp inspect the hook bait, attacking the feeder for each morsel of food and sending shimmers through the main line.

An angler next door then hooks and lands a cracking-looking common off the top and gets Jan thinking that his float-legering approach may not be best suited to these conditions.

"I've normally found the float to be most effective in dull conditions when a wind is rippling the surface. This will keep their heads down and feeding on the lake bed. Today, due to the warm temperatures and bright sunshine, the carp may be travelling in the upper layers of the water, which may not suit this style. I'll give it a few hours, but if nothing occurs I may go stalking for a while on the lake behind us," he comments.

The disturbance on the feeder then comes to a halt, so Jan reels in and sets about refilling and recasting.

"Regular casting is imperative when incorporating a feeder, because it ensures that the swim is topped up with groundbait. This will keep the carp returning for more and hopefully induce them into sampling the hook bait.

"Float legering doesn't only lend itself to cage feeders, though. You can fish it with literally anything, from leads through to Method feeders. To be honest, any can be successful on the day – it totally depends on your baiting strategy."

With the temperature rising by the minute, Jan decides to reel in the rods and take a quick look at the lake behind us. Again, it's a small, intimate water, but holds many more features. Lily pads, overhanging trees and dense Norfolk

Natural baits such as casters are great carp food...

Pike floats suit float legering perfectly.

... especially when coupled with groundbait...

reeds provide the perfect sanctuary for wary carp and they must be in there somewhere.

We both walk around the whole lake peeking into the reeds and watching the lilies for any movement that could reveal a carp's presence. The lake is flat calm, but slightly high due to the rain it has received during the past few days. This may slow down the fishing as a result of the extra cold water.

On our second lap, a small back breaks the surface and sends shimmers across the pool. A black shape emerges from the lilies and bow waves across the middle. It looks like a reasonable fish too, a nice golden common of around the double-figure mark. With that in mind Jan rigs up a floater rod.

"I'm not the most competent floater angler in the world, but I'm more than happy to give it a try on this occasion. The other lake has been pretty slow today and I feel that it could be the sudden influx of cold water that's put paid to any action. With the odd carp mooching around slightly below the surface I feel I can tempt one into sampling a pop-up providing my cast is accurate."

Jan then superglues a whittled-down pop-up cube to the shank of the hook

## COMPACTING THE FEEDER

**1** Place a firm section of groundbait at the base of a cage feeder, like so.

**2** Follow this with a small handful of casters and sweetcorn kernels.

**3** Finally, plug the end of the feeder with another layer of groundbait.

and casts straight in front of the travelling common carp. It hurriedly swims towards the hook bait, tilts up, and its nose just breaks the surface. We hear the telltale slurp as it engulfs the mixer in one. There's no need to strike because it took it with extreme confidence, followed by a huge eruption on the surface as an angry carp powers its way towards the lily bed.

The hooked fish strips yards of line from the spool and muscles its way into the lilies. As the line grates and pings on the stems, Jan keeps the strain on and coaxes it free. Soon enough it's out in the open water, twisting and circling about 20 yards out. It sends boils and bubbles to the surface as it tries to shed the hook and evade capture but, following constant pressure, Jan slips the net under a stunning common.

"Blimey, that didn't take long did it mate!" exclaims Jan. "The cast was straight on its nose and it took instantly. It's a magnificent, scale-perfect common too, my favourite."

As it thrashes round in the margins Jan leaves it for a few moments to calm down. This saves it doing itself any harm by flipping on the mat and possibly damaging its fins.

As it begins to calm down, Jan hoists the beautifully coloured common onto the mat and removes the hook. The scales are then removed from his rucksack and placed into the arms of the unhooking mat. They ping around to 11lb and Jan's well pleased at the result, considering the amount of rain that has entered the fishery over the last few days.

The carp's magnificent rows of golden scales glisten in the sun and look stunning in the pics. It's in wonderful nick and, looking at the perfectly formed mouth, may never have been hooked before.

After returning it, Jan rigs up another floater and trots off to take a look in the far-bank reed beds. As he creeps into the swim closest to the Norfolk reeds, he spots the odd fish basking in the sun. They're just quietly sitting there, lazing in the afternoon heat.

Consequently, Jan flicks a few floaters towards them and they slowly edge forward to slurp them in one by one. The only problem is the denseness of the reed bed. There are stems and twigs, branches and bushes, which could make the landing of any fish nigh-on impossible.

Because of this, Jan decides not to fish and simply enjoys watching the carp happily feed on each mixer he flicks in. There's no point in fishing at all costs because you are never going to land them, and you could easily put the carp's welfare at risk.

"As much as I enjoy catching any size of carp, there's nothing I like better than to watch them happily go about their daily routine without the risk of getting caught. You can learn so much by simply observing them at close quarters. This will certainly stand you in good stead for future sessions," Jan explains, as another good-sized fish slurps in a mixer.

The next few hours pass without event and we decide to call it a day. Through some opportunist carping, Jan managed to bag a carp when most others were failing. On the right day, though, the float-legering technique could have caught plenty of fish. It's even worth trying it on a harder, less-commercial pit too, because most big carp won't have ever seen the method before. Give it a go, and catch yourself a new PB!

Carefully does it.

A pair of lips slurp in the mixer and Jan's in...

... and a pristine common is soon posing for the camera.

# Autumn

# After Hours

The days are getting shorter and the weather colder, but now's the time to bag up on short evening sessions. Here, BRIAN SKOYLES shows you how…

It's that time of year when you're looking forward to winter. Hmmm, I'll start again. Summer is drawing to a close, the nights are getting longer, but it's a great time to be fishing. That's more like it, and it's true.

Autumn evenings are a terrific time to catch carp. You can arrive at the water while it's still daylight, have a couple of hours stalking, stay an hour or two into dark and still be home in time to avoid a telling off from 'the boss'.

The four key elements to successful autumn stalking are; choice of venue, bait choice and application, mobility and tactics. I will cover each of these areas over the next few pages.

You can use loads of different baits when stalking.

Add Multimino and evaporated milk to your particles.

This style of fishing is strictly short session, so you need a venue that you can reach quickly and easily. Look for one that has plenty of obvious features, such as margin reeds, weed beds, overhanging trees and suchlike. This will make the choice of spots to target far easier.

You obviously need a water with scope to move around, but this isn't usually a problem because of the time that you are fishing. Waters that are rammed with anglers every weekend and throughout summer become quieter as autumn sets in. Numerous anglers see the evenings as too short to bother with, so this is your chance to catch a few bonus fish.

This style of angling is about having fun, not necessarily banking a monster, so look for venues with a good head of fish. I have four local waters that fit the bill. They are stocked with plenty of doubles and there's an outside chance of a twenty. The furthest one is 40 minutes away, there's good bankside access and it's full of features.

They way to get the most from these short sessions is to travel light and stay mobile. You might fish three or four swims in the time available, so you need the minimum of gear. One rod is fine, but I do tend to take two. Both are tackled up, usually at the car, with completely different presentations. I'll set one up with a float and the other with a leger. This allows me the option of fishing the method that will give me the best chance.

Other than that I carry a few spare rig bits, landing net, sling, mat and bait. Everything will go into a small rucksack/tackle bag and I'm off.

I will prebait a number of chosen spots at the start of the session. I walk around looking for likely stalking spots, such as

## THE LEGER RIG

**1** This is my favourite hook arrangement for all my stalking rigs.

**2** An inline Korda lead with a Shockleader sleeve is my choice...

**3** ...coupled with a home-made back lead four feet behind the lead.

I craft my own floats from dry reed stems.

Set up well back from the water's edge.

Just two minutes fishing on a prebaited spot brings instant success.

overhanging trees, marginal features and suchlike, and when I find one I introduce bait and then move on and repeat the process. I try to prebait at least three or four spots at the beginning of each session.

Two or three handfuls of pellets and/ or particles are all that's needed on each spot and I usually introduce half a dozen hook-bait samples too.

Having baited three or four spots I return to them in the same order that I baited them to watch for any signs of feeding fish. If there are no obvious signs in any of the spots then I will simply pick a spot, fish it and hope for the best.

My favourite particle for this style of angling is Hinders French Mix – yes, French Mix. It was originally designed to attract and hold fish on the big French waters, but it works brilliantly in this country as well. I have total confidence in its ability to attract and hold carp. I do boost it by adding a tin of evaporated milk and 100ml of Multimino. This puts a milky cloud in the water that the fish love. I use a simple pellet mix consisting of Nutrabaits Trigga Ice and Hinders Slicker 60s.

Hook baits for stalking can be kept simple and you'll only need a few. If you have a favourite boilie then that's fine, but don't rule out some of the tried-and-tested baits, such as sweetcorn, Peperami and naturals, particularly worms.

Stalking in the margins is fishing at its best. It's up close and personal, there's no messing about with buzzers and banksticks and there's no waiting for hours on end.

The set-ups that I use are simple. On my float rod I like a waggler-style float attached to the line using a Drennan float attachment. I don't use split shot as these can weaken the line. The hooklength is tied to the line via a ring swivel and a small quantity of rig putty moulded around the swivel – easy.

BIngo! A carp moves in on a baited margin spot.

The leger set-up is also very simple. Firstly, I slide my home-made back lead onto the line, followed by a small Korda Square Pear inline lead. I replace the lead's plastic insert with a Korda Shockleader sleeve. Then I tie on the hooklength and pull the top of the swivel into the Shockleader sleeve. I use home-made back leads because they're line friendly and can be adjusted to suit any situation.

I use the same style of rig for both set-ups because it works well. It's very basic, but one that I have complete confidence in. I'm a great fan of fluorocarbon and it's perfect for this situation. At one end is a Korda ring swivel and at the other a size 10 Korda Wide Gape or a size 9 Fox SSC. I use the palomar knot for reliability and strength on the fluorocarbon.

## THE FLOAT RIG

**1** The business end comprises my favourite stalking hooklength.

**2** I wrap rig putty around the hooklength ring swivel, leaving the ring exposed.

**3** Any standard, waggler-type floats are attached to a Drennan float adaptor.

**4** This allows the float to be attached to my main line using silicone tubing.

# MAKE YOUR OWN BACK LEAD

**1** Cut a 2cm length of tubing from an empty Biro refil, as shown here.

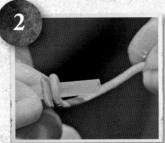

**2** Tightly wrap tungsten wire around the outside of the tubing.

**3** This is what you should end up with. You can alter the size and weight to suit.

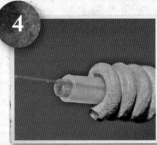

**4** Thread the back lead onto your line. Trap it in place with a piece of cocktail stick.

I whip a short length of Kryston Samson hair braid onto the shank of the hook to create a supple hair and protect it with a short piece of shrink tubing. I prefer this to tying a knotless knot with fluorocarbon because it allows the bait greater movement.

Using the same hooklength for both rigs means that I can sit and tie a couple at home, saving time on the bank.

## BUBBLES CAN BE UNRELIABLE, PARTICULARLY WHEN YOU'RE ONLY SEEING THE ODD ONE.

With this sort of fishing you can often see activity in your swim and there are three main types to look out for. The first is fish movement. This can be obvious in that you actually see the fish enter and exit the swim, but more often than not you'll see subtle signs. A reasonably big fish cannot move though the water without giving away its presence. If

you watch the water carefully you can sometimes see vortexes as the fish turns. It might not be much, but if you know what you are looking for it's a clear sign of fish activity.

The second giveaway is weed movement and this is usually easy to spot. Watch for pads twitching and reed stems that lean and move differently to the rest. Dense weed will often lift

slightly when a carp moves through it. These are all signs of fish in the swim.

The third sign, and my favourite, is bubbles. Not only do these mean that you have fish in the swim, but they are feeding too. The amount of bubbles can vary from the odd one or two to plate-sized eruptions of small bubbles. Bubbles can be unreliable, though, particularly when you're only seeing the odd one or two. These can be caused by plant gases, gas pockets in silt and suchlike, but with a bit of practice you can differentiate between these and bubbles caused by fish.

Having two different set-ups gives me the versatility to choose a rig depending on how the fish are feeding. If there's a lot of fish movement in the swim then

Stay low and avoid too much movement.

A great way of baiting accurately under foliage.

A scraper twenty, hooked just a few feet from the bank.

I'll use the leger set-up. The home-made back lead pins the line out of the way, meaning that I'm less likely to spook fish. If I have obvious bubbling in the swim or I'm fishing near snags or dense weed then I'll use the float because I receive a clearer picture from the float movement as to what is happening sub-surface. The other thing to bear in mind is that the leger can result in violent takes as the fish bolts. On the other hand, the float usually gives you slightly more warning. Those couple of seconds can be very important if you are fishing close to snags. Sometimes it is possible to efficiently and safely use both rods, with the leger to one side of the swim laid on the floor with a slack clutch and the float to the other side.

Approaching and fishing the swim in the correct manner is vital. You are

Get out and make the most of the autumn evenings. You'll be glad you made the effort.

going to be fishing extremely close in, sometimes right under your rod tip, so get the approach wrong and you will spook all the fish. If this happens you might as well go home because you haven't got time to wait for them to return.

Move slowly, keep low and ensure that you remain well back from the edge. I tend to put my gear down well away from the swim before moving forward with just the rod and a few baits. Once I am at the water's edge I pause and watch

My home-made rig dropper...

...which I use to place my baited rig under marginal bushes.

the swim before deciding exactly where to place my hook bait. Usually, lowering a bait into position or a gentle underhand swing is all that's required.

If you have fish in the swim then it can be difficult to place your bait without spooking them. You simply have to stay patient and wait for your chance.

If you really get into this style of fishing you can take things a little further and convert a pole into a hook-bait dropper, for accurately and quietly placing your rig, and use a bait spoon for baiting up.

The bait spoon is obvious, just buy one from a tackle shop and screw it to an extending landing-net pole. The hook-bait dropper you will have to make yourself. Mine consists of a rod blank with the rings removed, which cost £2 from a junk shop, with a small, bent piece of brass taped to the end. To use it, simply place the hair on your baited rig into the piece of brass, ship it out to your spot, twist the pole and out it slides.

Enter the twilight zone.

There's an expression that I use that was picked up from work training sessions that goes: "Don't try to work harder, try to work smarter." This could so easily be modified to cover autumn stalking – don't fish longer and harder, fish sharper.

With a bit of organisation and the minimum of effort, autumn evenings can provide fabulous short-session fishing, so why don't you get out there and give it a try.

# OPEN-WATER
# GOLD

STEVE RENYARD demonstrates his mastery of open-water fishing with an early autumn trip to CEMEX Angling's Papercourt.

To say that we're going in blind would be an understatement. We know that the biggest fish present, Shoulders, has been over 40lb in the past and there are one or two other impressive specimens present. That's it. Far from being nervous about putting his reputation on the line, Steve is buzzing: "I've been really looking forward to this trip since we decided on Papercourt. It's like stepping back into my carp fishing past. Apart from one fish, the whole stock is a big mystery – there might even be uncaught carp in here – it's the most exciting fishing that I've had for six or seven years."

CEMEX Papercourt, so the guidebook tells us, is 32 acres. As we stand in the car park Steve notes that it looks a fair bit bigger, stretching away to our left and right. The venue is steep banked with a sailing club at one end and a couple of feature-heavy bays at the other. It's clear that Papercourt is suffering from a lack of water because it seems a long way below normal levels. It's Friday afternoon and Steve has been here for an hour or so already and has started to formulate a plan after seeing fish roll a couple of swims down from the car park.

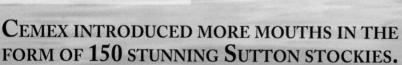

## CEMEX INTRODUCED MORE MOUTHS IN THE FORM OF 150 STUNNING SUTTON STOCKIES.

Steve gives his first impressions of the lake as we settle down for the evening. "Papercourt certainly isn't overfished, although there are a few anglers on. There doesn't seem to be any snag fishing or real close-in fishing to be done here. There aren't many originals in here so the thought of catching one for the cameras is really exciting. The only snippet of tactical information that we've been able to dig up is that many of the locals use bait boats. That means that they'll probably be using particles and a few boilies. I've had a chat with a bailiff and he told me that single hook baits are also

a favoured tactic. This plays right into my hands because I'm going to do just the opposite. I'm going to use 18mm baits to change the feeding pattern of fish out there. I'm sure that they're used to taking their time and not moving very far while feeding over particles. They can't take so much time with boilies – there simply isn't as much bait there and competition will only serve to increase the speed of consumption! The bigger fish in here will need to eat plenty to keep their energy levels up, especially as CEMEX has recently introduced more mouths in the form of 150 stunning Sutton stockies.

I haven't changed the bait from the last session; I'm still on the Richworth Crab & Mussel that I had a 32lb common on last time out. I've managed another nine thirties on the bait, so confidence is high.

Steve explains his swim choice as he settles into a comfortable, beach-like swim surrounded by fruiting brambles and dog rose.

"There was a lovely swim down by the car park that initially took my

fancy. It was at the bottom of a steep bank and commanded an area of water that contained a few gravel humps and silkweed-covered shallows. Bearing in mind that we're expecting a warm, high-pressure weekend it would have been a decent choice. However, I noticed one or two subtle rolls out between a few buoys to the left of the car-park swim. When I wandered down here I saw a couple more turn on the surface and my mind was made up. Since heaving my gear down here I've been doing a little investigating. I've overcast the marker float and tentatively run it through a few times. I found depths between nine and 12 feet over a sandy lake bed. I've decided that I am going to fish all three rods in the area immediately out in front, between the buoys where the fish were rolling. Initially, I'm only going to put out stringers, trying to ambush a fish. I've always been fascinated by drawing

After seeing a couple of fish roll, swim choice was easy.

the attention of fish to the hook bait and the round stringer is the best way. This focusing onto the situation around the hook bait is key in open-water fishing. A six-bait stringer fished like this is difficult for a fish to miss as it browses the open water."

## I'M HAPPY TO KEEP APPLYING THE BAIT AS I THINK THAT THE NATURAL FOOD IS ON THE WANE.

After a few biteless hours Steve needs to prepare his area for the night. He's considering baiting fairly widely.

"Although I can't explain it, I think that the fish want to be in this area so I've decided to scatter 1.5kg of bait over the area to try and keep them here. By scattering the baits widely I'm hoping to create a different baiting situation than would be possible with a bait boat. It's a bit of a gamble but 1.5kg spread over three rods isn't much. People seem to worry about putting plenty of bait in but if you went out there and tried to find all the baits again you'd struggle to half fill your bag! On a big pit like this you do need to pull fish in. You might not stop them but if they hang around long enough to get caught you'll have had a result. At this time of year I am more than happy to keep applying the bait because I think that the natural food is on the wane."

Just as an incredible golden sunrise is strengthening in the east, Steve is away on his left-hand rod. A tense scrap

Ambush tactics – Steve starts with stringers alone.

unfolds in front of the smouldering sky before Steve nets a powerfully built common in immaculate condition. It's a fantastic result to end the first night of our stay and Steve is understandably pleased!

As the day progresses it becomes clear that not everything is going to plan. One after another sailing boats appear in front of Steve until he decides to reel in.

"As you'll see from the pictures, the boats are now out in force," says Steve. "We've counted 48!

"CEMEX does recommend that you back lead," Steve notes, "but I've taken the chance to rest my swim during the hottest part of the day because the boats are coming pretty close to the bank. After talking to the bailiff it seems that Papercourt isn't an easy water but it's definitely an intriguing one and I'm enjoying every minute."

Tough line for the rigours of gravel-pit fishing

Pro Clear

A cracking Papercourt common in the early morning mist.

Always take good care of them.

Steve rested his swim during the busiest part of the day!

The icing on the cake – a Papercourt upper twenty.

Marker work is essential for open-water fishing.

Crab & Mussel proved its worth once more.

Steve battles a beast out in the fog.

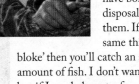
It's all the buoy's fault!

It's 7pm when the boats sail back and Steve fills us in on his latest move.

"I wasn't sure whether to put more bait out but I've ended up putting out another 1kg. I'm that confident that the Crab & Mussel will get eaten."

Because the boats have disturbed the swim during the day, Steve isn't worried about getting the marker float out again and he's had a result.

"I've found an area rising from 12 feet to eight feet. I've run the marker float over it three times and I'm sure that it's a mussel bed, and the abundance of broken shells on the bank seems to suggest that I could be right. That is precisely the type of thing that I'm looking for, especially seeing as the rest of the area is fairly uniform sandy lake bed."

Steve marks up his rod before settling in for his second night full of anticipation and wakes suddenly before first light.

"I woke up for no reason and sat up wide awake," he later tells me. "I must have been sitting there for two minutes drinking in the cool early hours' air when I had some action. It was a bit of a funny take – at first I thought that it was a liner. The bobbin rose and resettled before absolutely ripping off. The fish gave another great tussle in the deep water, fighting for around 15 minutes. It turned out to be a 26lb 14oz original common. There wasn't a mark in its mouth. I'm completely chuffed, two originals on your first visit is really good going apparently."

As we're finishing the photos Steve's middle rod melts off. He's forced to back wind as well as giving line through the clutch as a beast of a fish battles out in the thick fog. With visibility down to less than 30 yards, Steve realises too late that the fish is going to make the other side of a buoy. Because the water is deep his line angle seemed to suggest that the fish was safely his side of the buoy. It's soon stuck fast and despite showing a great deal of patience Steve soon reels in a broken hook link – at least the fish is away. Understandably, he's not happy.

"I haven't felt so gutted about losing a fish since my Withy Pool days; I'm gutted."

It proves that single hook baits aren't the only answer on these big pits. Don't just fish the way that everyone else does – if you're on a big water like Papercourt and you have boilies at your disposal, try scattering them. If you do the same thing as 'average bloke' then you'll catch an average amount of fish. I don't want to preach but if I can help put a few open-water carp on the bank for you then job done!

# GET SERIOUS – GET SOME SERIOUS HELP!

The magazine for the ultra-dedicated angler obsessed by carp and carp fishing. Featuring the biggest names, the biggest fish and the biggest stories.

## ON SALE THE SECOND MONDAY OF EACH MONTH

**ADVANCED CARP FISHING**

BIG-CARP FISHING'S No1 READ!

WIN £1,559 WORTH OF PRIZES INCLUDING A FULL FOX LONG-RANGE SET-UP

£3.50 NOVEMBER 2008    DHP

**RANGEMASTER**
Revealed: the leads that fly further

**BEAT THE BAN**
Leadcore banned? Try Jim Shelley's hybrid

**CRITICAL EDGES**
Martin Pick cracks Sandhurst on wafters

**EXPERIMENTAL CARPING**

Nick Helleur explains how making tactical changes to your rigs will help you bank more big carp this autumn

**NEW-RIG SUCCESS**
Steve Renyard bags a 37lb mirror on his latest creation

**INTO THE UNKNOWN**
ACF visits the northern venue that could hold uncaught giants

DISCOVER HOW MATT GOSLING BANKED A FORTY-POUNDER INCHES FROM THE BANK

# STRING 'EM ALONG

Total Carp editor MARC COULSON explains how a bag of boilies and some PVA string is all you need to catch a few autumn carp.

The stringers prove their worth as a common carp kisses the spreader block.

**W**hat I am trying to prove in this piece is twofold. Firstly, that you really don't have to use lots of baits in order to catch fish and, secondly, that the age-old tactic of PVA stringers is still a useful and effective one.

I used to read about stringers all the time and it was a tactic that I employed a lot during my early days trying to catch carp. Then, as with so many other carp anglers, they soon disappeared from my radar. I put it down to the advent of PVA mesh. This allowed all manner of new presentations to be experimented with, from the original stuff, through to the boilie type that pretty much replaced stringers. A few boilies squeezed into the narrow-mesh PVA created a stringer with a difference. They were tightly packed into the PVA and, once the mesh melted, the boilies exploded from the PVA. This left a random pile of three, four or five boilies around the hook bait and many anglers wrote that this was better than the predictable line of baits left when using a conventional stringer. I have to be honest and say that I fell for it all hook, line and sinker.

## STRING OR TAPE?

Putting aside bags and mesh, there are still several types of PVA available. I prefer to use the tape-style PVA during winter and cooler water conditions, with string being my choice when it's warmer. Basically, I feel more confident in the tape's ability to melt fully when the water is cold.

Then, along came the likes of Dave Gawthorn, Steve Spurgeon and Nick Helleur with their varied, and often ingenious, uses of mesh PVA, including the now famous groundbait stick. Some, partly due to its shape and partly due to the fact that the 'some' were Dynamite Baits-sponsored anglers, christened it the Dynamite Stick. Whatever, I, like a host of other carp anglers, used it with

all manner of groundbait mixes, so the Dynamite bit was soon dropped from the title as far as I was concerned.

So, a few years on and we all use PVA in many different ways. However, I got to thinking recently that the humble stringer is often maligned and certainly misunderstood by many. For many more it is simply neglected. This neglect can maintain the tactic's effectiveness and those who do use it can reap the rewards.

I have fallen back in love with stringers and if I only had one tactic to use anywhere it would have to be the following:

STEP ONE: Tie a reliable and effective rig
STEP TWO: Add a good-quality boilie hook bait
STEP THREE: Tie up and attach a five-bait stringer of matching boilies
STEP FOUR Cast out and catapult another 10 to 15 baits in the vicinity

So, yes, stringers are very much back in favour as far as I am concerned and I now use them on at least one rod on every trip. However, there are a few things to bear in mind when using them, because failure to use stringers correctly can result in you experiencing more than a few problems.

Firstly, don't make them too long. Stringers are not the easiest things to cast at the best of times, and certainly cut down on the aerodynamics of your rig. The more baits you add, the more this is exaggerated.

You MUST use a decent-quality PVA string or tape. I favour string during

**Five-bait stringers – the editor's choice.**

Couple your stringers with effective rigs.

## CAUGHT ON CAMERA!

**1** Marc lands another common as the Total Carp film crew arrives.

**2** The fish goes 20lb 8oz and Marc is well pleased.

**3** Get yourself on to www.totalcarpmagazine.com for the full story.

summer, such as Gardner's original (this is two-ply so I unravel it first to use one strand) and Kryston Meltdown, although there are plenty of others out there. In winter I still use stringers but change to a narrow PVA tape, such as Kryston Melt-Ex or Korda Kwik Melt. I have found that, for some reason, the tape melts better and more consistently in colder water.

Another must-do is to leave a slight gap between each bait. This allows the water into the string or tape and guarantees that it melts. I have seen PVA contract quite badly in water, especially cold water, before it starts to melt. If there is no gap between your baits this can be an absolute nightmare. This gap is easy to create with boilies because the baits tend to grip the PVA and stay where they are. If you are using, say, tiger nuts, it is often a good idea to add a small chunk of PVA foam between each bait to keep them separated.

Finally, stringers can be a good way of avoiding rig tangles, but you must feather your cast, and quite positively at that. This allows the rig and stringer to straighten out before hitting the water and can be the difference between an effective presentation and a right mess!

So, that just about cover stringers and why I think that you should use, or at least try, them. A key bonus is that you can fish this tactic with only a small amount of bait. This, for me, is ideal because the waters that I fish are quite busy and I never know what bait is already out there in front of my

"I love it when a plan comes together!"

swim. By this, I mean that the angler in the swim before me, and the one before them, could easily have put a bit of bait out. To bait on top of bait is, to my mind at least, a mistake. Like the match anglers say: "You can put more in but you cannot take it out." By fishing stringers and a few supplementary boilies you can actually make use of whatever bait is out there. If there is in fact no bait already in the swim then the stringer is still a valid approach.

All this theory is all well and good, you might say, but can I prove that it actually

Absolutely chuffed with a new PB common; proving that stringers definitely still do the business!

Once the sling was deducted the common went 26lb 4oz.

# HOW TO TIE MARC'S SIMPLE STRINGERS

**1** A packet of PVA string will last you ages, making this a cheap tactic indeed.

**2** Thread the baits one by one onto a stringer needle. Marc favours the gated type.

**3** He always uses five baits in his stringers. "It's a confidence thing," he says.

**4** Marc unravels the two-ply Gardner PVA to make it last even longer. He's so tight!

**5** Loop the PVA over and hook it onto the stringer needle, as shown.

**6** Pull the baits off the needle and onto the PVA string. Don't break the baits.

**7** Always leave a slight gap between the baits so that the water melts the PVA.

**8** Loop the end of the PVA string onto the hook on your baited rig.

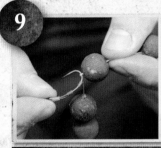

**9** Pull the top bait up to the hook to trap the stringer in place.

**10** Push a piece of PVA foam onto the point of the hook, as shown here.

**11** Add a second piece of foam like so. This stops the hair tangling on the cast.

**12** Ready to go. Marc would cast his stringers out on most lakes. Try 'em yourself.

works? Well, I set out on a recent session to do exactly that, armed with just my rods and reels and suchlike, 1kg of boilies and some PVA string. The aim was to use this favourite tactic to catch and hopefully take some boilies and most of the string home afterwards.

The trip could not have gone better and I managed two commons, including my PB common carp at 26lb 4oz. The second fish, which weighed 20lb 8oz, was even caught live for the Total Carp website cameras (go to *www. totalcarpmagazine.com*). I used about ½kg of boilies – in this case Nash Scopex Squid Livers with Robin Red – and, I imagine, about six feet of PVA string. There was certainly enough left in the pack to go back and do it all over again. Oh, and I lost a carp too.

So, three bites, including a PB common, on very little bait and some PVA; I bet most of you reading this

would take that for a day's fishing. I was certainly extremely happy, not only with the fish but with the fact that I had proved that the PVA stringer, my favourite tactic, had come up trumps. You know what, it won't be the last time either and I cannot wait to get back out there and use them all over again. You should try them too – you might just be glad that you did.

**Catapult a dozen or so baits over the top of your stringers.**

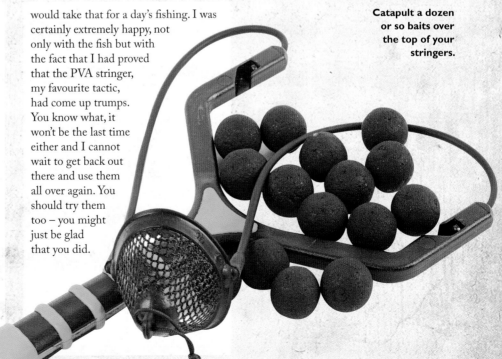

# SPECIES HUNT

We join ADAM PENNING on the banks of Chilham Mill as he bids to catch different species of carp. This time he targets the mirrors.

Mirrors are probably my favourite of all the carp species. They all possess various characteristics that stand them out. It may be a small cluster of starburst scales or a row of linear plates that makes them unique and that's what I find so appealing.

weather warning predicted for the early hours in the morning. They've also forecast several inches of snow over the next few days and subzero temperatures – not ideal conditions!

The water is gin clear due to the colder weather and bird life is prevalent. Every time I try to introduce a free offering

## EVERY TIME I TRY TO INTRODUCE A FREE OFFERING IT'S POUNCED ON.

I've been lucky enough to cradle some magnificent mirror carp and they never cease to amaze me. The Oxfordshire strains are truly remarkable and I've managed to land some stunning fish from the popular Chilham Mill Fishery in Kent. I really did have a couple of sessions to remember, landing no less than 28 fish, with five of them breaking the magical 30lb barrier.

So that's where you find me today, bivvied up in the reputable Bailiff's Island swim. The weather is absolutely dire, with northerly winds and a severe

it's pounced on by a seagull or diving tuftie. The only way to get around it is by spodding during the hours of darkness or through PVA-bag work.

I'm currently located to the left of Bailiffs Island with large expanses of open water in front of me. The shaded water surrounding the

A hard-fighting mirror is drawn to the net.

Nailed on the trusty maggot-ball hook bait.

The action was pretty regular.

A perfect carp-attracting spot.

island is infested with weed, which makes presentation pretty difficult, so I'm steering clear of that area. I do like to fish near dead weed, though, because carp pick off natural food items from the dying stems and roots. Due to the abnormal winter that we've encountered the weed simply hasn't died back, putting the fish into a bit of a quandary. It's basically given them the chance to feed heavily when they'd normally be lying torpid and grouped together in the most comfortable part of the lake.

At the beginning of the session, I briefly explored the lake bed with the marker rod and found the main area covered in light silt, with scatterings of weed and chod. This is exactly what I'm looking for during winter, as prominent gravel bars and humps are a lot shallower than I'd like, and sometimes more pressured so carp often avoid them. The majority of this lake is around four to five feet deep and I have managed to find a slightly deeper trough at around six and a half feet, which is the ideal winter feeding spot.

With my chosen spot sorted I accurately cast two hook baits each side of the marker float. I then clipped up the spod rod to the correct distance ready to introduce some bait as the light began to fade. This would prevent any bait-stealing critters gorging themselves on my offerings.

I successfully introduced my spod concoction, consisting mainly of my favourite winter bait – maggots! Just to give them a bit of extra spice I added some Activ-8 liquid and some Roach

groundbait. The maggots absorb the groundbait and flavours and reek of the trademark smell. If I burst a maggot it would ooze flavour – it was extraordinary and I'm sure that it gave me an edge.

## THE MAJORITY OF TAKES IN MY PAST FEW SESSIONS WERE OVER LARGE BEDS OF MAGGOTS.

The spod mix was kept simple because I wanted the carp to be seeking out small food items, as opposed to the whole boilies they find day in, day out. Maggots fit the bill perfectly! I even avoided using bright corn, pellets and hemp because they look far too obvious over a bed of maggots and scream out danger.

After spodding several pints of maggots accurately over my spots, I had

The scales say it all.

to contemplate where I was going to cast the third rod. I'd found a nice clean spot earlier in the day, so the decision was made easily. Again, I cast a maggot hook bait and PVA bag to the area. It landed

with a satisfying thud and I was to keep this fished on its own, without any free offerings. I didn't want to put all of my eggs into one basket. I was fishing two over a bed of bait and one on its own. That way I'd get a fair idea of what the fish were craving. The majority of the takes I received in my past few sessions were all over large beds of maggots, so I was confident that one of them would rattle off at some point.

With all three rods sorted I sat back confident of some action, even though the weather was totally against us. It gave me time to reflect on my recent success.

My most successful sessions came during the unseasonably mild December period. It was wet and the wind was blowing strong southwesterlies for the majority of my stay. This really turned the carp on and each evening I would observe fish as they head and tailed over my baited areas. I'd see the occasional huge lump crashing and relishing the warm temperatures; I just knew something would happen. Adrenaline was pumping through my body and I found it hard to sleep that first night. I stayed on for three days and by the

Note how the hook bait stands out.

I like to add a little groundbait to the mix for added attraction.

end I was so fatigued that I slept for almost a whole day. My tactics were obviously spot on and I managed to land 13 carp to over 30lb. What a start and that whetted my appetite for more! At the end of the session I introduced the leftover maggots, mixed with a healthy sprinkling of chopped Grange boilies and I couldn't wait to return.

I returned the following week armed with a bucketful of maggots and some more chopped Grange boilies. The water

was extremely clear but the conditions were similar to that of the last trip, with warm winds and rain.

As far as tactics were concerned, I tried to be different from the norm, just like the session before. Chilham is an extremely pressured water and the carp have seen it all. They are under a constant barrage from some of the UK's finest anglers, making them wily creatures. So, with clued-up carp and gin-clear water I yet again had my work cut out.

Consequently, I had to come up with some sort of strategy and bitty baits such as maggots, coupled with blending in my end tackle, were to be my major focal point. To prevent the carp spooking on my main line, I had spooled up with low-diameter fluorocarbon. When it comes into contact with water you can barely see it, making it the ideal line. I coupled the fluorocarbon with a clear Safe Zone leader and my end tackle would appear almost invisible. To pin

## FINING-DOWN TACTICS

**1** Peel off 14 inches of IQ Xtra Soft fluorocarbon, which is practically invisible in water.

**2** Creat a small hair loop and thread on a tiny piece of fine silicone tubing.

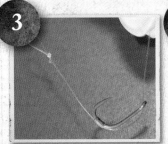

**3** Thread the hook through the silicone so that the rig now looks like this.

**4** Whip the fluorocarbon to the hook with a knotless knot. Moisten and then draw tight.

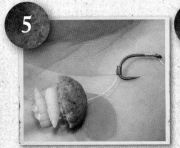

**5** Thread half a boilie and two glow-in-the-dark imitation maggots onto the hair.

**6** Carefully whittle down the boilie to create a disc-shaped bait. Small but very attractive.

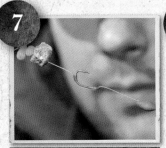

**7** Add a piece of tungsten putty to the rig in this position. You're nearly there.

**8** The final rig should be about 12 inches long once tied to your chosen swivel and lead set-up.

The first frosts were pretty dramatic at times.

them down further I added a large blob of tungsten putty. I'm sure the extra thought of blending everything in landed me some bonus fish.

Following the success on my first trip, I decided to keep tactics pretty similar. The first fish that I landed on my second session was a mid-twenty mirror. It was caught on the trusted maggot-ball hook baits and excreted Grange boilies all over the unhooking mat. This told me two things – they were eating the chopped Grange baits in quantity and to save time I could probably get away with changing to chopped-boilie hook baits and a couple of rubber maggots.

To maximise the length of time my baits were in the water, I tied up some spare rigs with a chopped-boilie hook bait and two rubber maggots attached.

## BY MORNING I WAS LEFT THINKING THAT I COULD HAVE ENTICED A FEW MORE.

Due to the water clarity and sly nature of the carp my hooklength material was also completely fined down. So, light, 8lb fluorocarbon was used as a hooklength. Now you may be thinking that I must be mad to use such a light material, but with balanced tackle you'd be amazed at what you can get away with. The abrasion resistance is superb and although many of the fish I hooked were deep in weed beds, all you need to do is apply constant pressure and ease them out. It's a lot stronger than you think and I'm positive that it's the fining down that creates more bites. I'd much prefer to play the fish more carefully on light tackle, rather than use heavy coated hook links and not receive the take in the first place. I did use longer hooklengths than normal too, with 12in lengths being common. This was to ensure that they settled on the silt

and dead weed rather than burying and disappearing out of sight.

I'm an avid user of smaller hooks, too. All my fish during those trips fell to a size 10 Korda Wide Gape. The hooks were firmly embedded in the bottom lip and never looked liked pulling!

Returning the last of the campaign's mirrors. I can't wait to go back!

That night I managed to land a few more fish, but by morning I was left thinking that I could have enticed a few more. At 2am, while I was lying in the bag, I listened to the huge boshes created by airborne carp landing and couldn't understand why I wasn't receiving much action. I decided that I'd have to change something for the following night.

With that in mind, I altered the rigs I'd previously tied and tipped the whittled-down boilie with two glow-in-the dark maggots. I don't think the standard versions were doing a good enough job and I began to think that I could have enticed more pick-ups.

My lead set-up was again focused on the ultra-sensitive aspect. Cold-water carp often feed slower and the slightest bleep on the buzzer can indicate a take. That's why I opted to use free-running, inline leads. To form the rig, I simply remove the insert from a Korda inline lead and thread it onto a leader.

That night my focused thoughts on the little changes paid dividends. My little glow-in-the dark maggots were

Every one of my Chilham carp were stunners...

... includng this chap with his recognisable tail...

... this one with its sparsely scaled flanks...

This near-leather was a real character fish.

... and this absolute cracker.

inducing more takes than usual and by the morning I'd landed seven or eight fish with a couple of thirties, too. It's the small changes that make the big differences and I felt that I had finally gone one step ahead of the carp. I actually felt guilty towards the end of that session because I was continually asking my mate, Tom, who was fishing next to me, to photograph the carp that I was catching and he looked completely shattered.

The more fish that I caught, the more confident I was becoming and I started to experiment after a while. I began lengthening my hairs and finally came up with one that nailed them perfectly almost every single time. It was surprising how just a small change in hair length affected the hook-holds. I also tampered with the silicone tubing, moving it around the bend of the hook to more of an aggressive angle. The experimentation has certainly opened my eyes and I really feel this winter has dramatically improved my overall angling ability.

By fining down I have been able to induce more takes and I'm certainly going to be keeping a close eye on how the match anglers fish. They definitely know how to get a bite when the odds are stacked against them and I am of the belief that their tactics have a lot to offer the carp angler who is targeting specimen fish.

By the end of that second three-day session I managed to land a staggering 15 fish. It was amazing and I shall never overlook fining down again, that's for sure!

This last session wasn't anything to write home about, though. After a top-notch curry I hit the sack but the weather took a turn for the worse with freezing temperatures and the lake went as flat as a millpond. When I woke in the morning I peered out of the bivvy and noticed some cat ice in the margins. My reels were frozen solid and coated with frost and my lines were brittle. I then tried picking up one of the rods for a recast and found that half of the lake had frozen solid – great!

We agreed that it would be awesome to catch a fish in such conditions, but we also knew that we were kidding ourselves and I finally gave in to the elements – my first blank on Chilham Mill this winter!

Oh well, you can't control the weather and I'd been lucky in previous sessions. I'm certainly going to apply fluorocarbon into my fishing more because its qualities are second to none. It's not going to be something that I only use in winter either, because summer fish can be just as wary. Give it a try, your results are sure to dramatically improve!

# Winter

# WHY WINTER?

GARETH FAREHAM grabs his gear and enough bait for a day session before setting out to show you why winter is one of the best times of year to catch carp...

For those of you who hang up your rods for the winter season, let me tell you that you're missing out on some great sport. I absolutely love fishing in the winter. In fact, it's one of my favourite times.

First of all, the banks have far less anglers on them and this means a greater choice of swims, fewer lines in the water and plenty of peace and quiet. Secondly, the fish are almost always in better condition.

They're in their winter colours and are usually a bit bigger than during summer. There's just something amazing about catching a big carp on a lovely frosty morning.

The key to success through winter is, without doubt, venue choice. If you choose the wrong venue, then you are going to struggle for bites and that's not nice, even when the weather's warm. Try to find a venue that fishes right through the winter.

Most waters have a spell of a couple of months or so when they shut up shop and the carp seemingly disappear. However, by doing a little bit of homework you can usually find a productive winter venue. For example Billinge, where I'm fishing today, is one of the few waters in the area that produces consistently throughout the colder months.

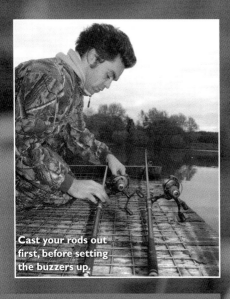

Cast your rods out first, before setting the buzzers up.

## CONCEAL YOUR LINE

**1**

Back leads are specifically designed to pin your main line to the lake bed.

**2**

Using quality, sinking leaders will pin down the line close to your rig.

**3**

Place a blob of rig putty on the end of the leader; this keeps it on the bottom.

**4**

Fish slack lines with the previous steps to ensure that your line is concealed.

What you're looking for in a winter water, or at least what I look for, is a good winter track record and a decent head of carp. By selecting quite a small venue you're never that far away from the fish. Ideally, the water won't be too deep either. I have found that shallower venues tend to be more productive in winter because the water warms up far quicker than on deep venues, which has a huge impact on how the carp behave.

Bait going into the venue on a regular basis is definitely a big help. You don't need a lot. If I'm fishing a venue regularly, then I'll try to get down to the lake at least a couple of times a week and spread maybe 1kg, or even just a few handfuls of bait, over a few areas. As soon as that bait stops going in, you're fighting a losing battle.

It tends to be boilies that I bait up with, such as one of the winterised Mainline baits, Grange or Active Maple-8, to keep the fish searching for food. I steer clear of particles and pellets. Hemp is the only exception to this, but I class hemp as different bait to other particles.

When I talk about particles, I mean things like Partiblend, Red Band and suchlike. I do like using hemp, it's perfect for keeping the carp in a certain area and, being black, is fairly inconspicuous in the clear water, plus it's relatively birdproof! If you want to keep the fish in a specific swim for a couple of days, then a few kilos of hemp will work a treat.

I keep my winter fishing to short day sessions so long as I'm fishing somewhere local. I'll go for just a couple of hours, adopting a hit-and-run style. The time of day I fish depends entirely on the bite times for that particular water.

**Recast regularly if you've had no action.**

## GAZ'S ULTRA-EFFECTIVE WINTER RIG

**1** These are the components that I use for tying my favourite winter rig.

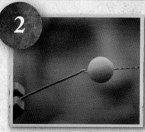

**2** Thread a 10mm or 8mm pop-up onto a length of Sink Link.

**3** Tie on a small rig ring below the bait, using two overhand knots.

**4** The ring needs to be just a few millimetres away from the bait.

**5** Tie a size 10 long-shanked hook to the braid with a knotless knot.

**6** Tie the braid to a length of IQ fluorocarbon using the knot detailed overleaf.

**7** Put a length of shrink tubing onto the hook. Note the length of the braid.

**8** Shrink the tubing and bend to a 45-degree angle with the hook shank.

**9** Place a blob of rig putty over the knot. You're now ready to catch carp.

For instance, last year the productive time on this venue was between 12pm and 2pm, so I'd turn up at 11am and leave at 3pm. It's a great way to fish; you can be home for dinner, you've not had to spend hours on end out in the cold, yet you've still fished the most productive time of the day, which is the important thing.

Obviously, the bite times will vary from water to water and you'll need to find the productive time on your chosen venue to do this, but it's well worth it.

While a lot of my local fishing is done in this hit-and-run style, I keep a campaign going on a big-fish water. I'll spend most of this winter as I did last year, on Park Lake in Wiltshire. Because of the distance I have to travel to get to Park Lake, it's pointless going for a quick day session. Because of this I'll aim to do two or, ideally, three days at a time. Obviously, this is a bit more time-consuming and you have to take more kit, but I really enjoy it, and there's no shortcut to catching the big fish, and you do have to put the time in.

It will come as no surprise that the weather conditions have a massive influence on how productive your session is likely to be. If I'm just going for an afternoon or a morning, then I'll try and time it to coincide with some favourable weather.

The ideal weather conditions are a bit of a contentious issue, but I favour days when there's a bit of sun around. I like using small, bright baits and they tend to work better when there's a bit of sun penetrating the water. I've never done that well on dull, windy days.

**Take plenty of pre-tied rigs with you.**

# SHIMANO TRIBAL XTREME

Constructed using ultra-rugged 3000 Denier material and packed full of features, the Tribal Xtreme luggage is an extensive range of purpose built waterproof and highly durable luggage - backed by a 2 year guarantee.

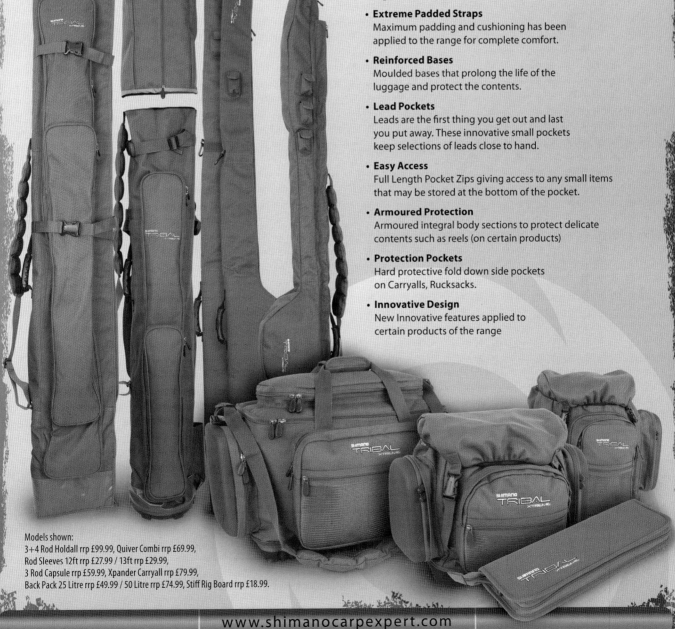

- **Highest Quality Body Materials**
  Durable, high quality poly backed 3000 denier material which is 100% waterproof.

- **Fittings**
  Highest Quality Zips, Tags & Fittings.

- **Extreme Padded Straps**
  Maximum padding and cushioning has been applied to the range for complete comfort.

- **Reinforced Bases**
  Moulded bases that prolong the life of the luggage and protect the contents.

- **Lead Pockets**
  Leads are the first thing you get out and last you put away. These innovative small pockets keep selections of leads close to hand.

- **Easy Access**
  Full Length Pocket Zips giving access to any small items that may be stored at the bottom of the pocket.

- **Armoured Protection**
  Armoured integral body sections to protect delicate contents such as reels (on certain products)

- **Protection Pockets**
  Hard protective fold down side pockets on Carryalls, Rucksacks.

- **Innovative Design**
  New Innovative features applied to certain products of the range

Models shown:
3+4 Rod Holdall rrp £99.99, Quiver Combi rrp £69.99,
Rod Sleeves 12ft rrp £27.99 / 13ft rrp £29.99,
3 Rod Capsule rrp £59.99, Xpander Carryall rrp £79.99,
Back Pack 25 Litre rrp £49.99 / 50 Litre rrp £74.99, Stiff Rig Board rrp £18.99.

www.shimanocarpexpert.com

Even if there's a good wind, like a southwesterly, I don't like it to be too strong because I don't think strong winds in winter are conducive to good fishing. If it is really windy, then the back of it is always worth a go.

On the other hand, if I'm going for a few days then, although I'll check the weather forecast, I won't let poor conditions deter me. After all, if you're not at the lake you can't catch.

When the water's as clear as it is here today, I pin as much of my main line and leader to the lake bed as I can. At the moment I'm using Korda's Safe Zone leaders, which sink like bricks and have a couple of small, tungsten weights built onto them. I have a small blob of putty at the end of the leader and back leads and slack lines. I've always found that it makes a massive difference to get everything pinned down, so I do everything that I can and especially on small, pressured venues.

The fluorocarbon hooklength falls into the same category of rig concealment. I'm not a fan of the massively overdone camouflaged rig components, such as heavily textured leads, tubing and hooks with bits stuck onto them and all that.

See, I told you winter could be productive.

Obviously, I want my end tackle to be as inconspicuous as possible, but I'm not convinced about the latest camou rig bits. Maybe, if you're after ultra-shy carp in gin-clear, shallow water, it might help – but for 99.9 per cent of angling situations it's pointless.

More often than not, on short/day sessions I'll fish a small, 10mm or 12mm pop-up or balanced bottom bait. Either a Heathrow Bait Services Indian Spice pop-up or one of my small, yellow citrus-flavoured home-made baits. Unfortunately, I can't tell you what's in them otherwise I'd have to kill you! These are fished either on their own or with a tiny PVA bag.

The problem with PVA bags is that even a small one can look glaringly obvious. If you're using a stick mix, pellets or something similar, as it lightens you'll get a coaster or CD-sized spread of light-coloured bait that can stand out a mile.

Quite often I'll be casting regularly as well. I don't want to leave big piles of bait everywhere so the smaller the bag,

Watch the water. Any signs of carp are a big advantage in locating winter hide-outs.

## GAZ'S BRAID/MONO COMBI-LINK KNOT, EXPLAINED

**1** Fold the end of the fluorocarbon over and pass the braid through the loop formed. Note the position of the hook.

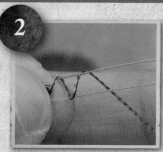

**2** Hold the eye of the hook and the fluorocarbon. Wrap the braid around the loop, as shown here, eight times.

**3** Wind the braid back down the loop, over the top of the previous coils, four times. Pass the tag end through the loop.

**4** Moisten the braid and gently pull the knot tight. You should be left with a knot like this. Trim the tag ends and it's job done.

Small bags and baits – spot on.

## BE MOBILE – MINIMISE YOUR KIT

**1** A rucksack holds everything that I'm going to need for a day session, including my unhooking mat.

**2** A small quiver takes my rods, a landing net and a brolly. It's lightweight and easy to carry.

**3** A chair is the only other item that I take. Being comfortable is important during winter.

the better. If you only use tiny amounts of bait, then you'll have no hesitation in moving swims either, which is a massive part of winter carping.

If your time on the bank is limited, as it is on short winter sessions, you have to stay alert. Keep watching the water for any visual signs that might tell you where the carp are. Bubbling, fish head and shouldering or crashing out are quite obvious signs that you need to look out for.

Because they're not as active in winter you have to find the fish. Sometimes, being just 15 to 20 yards away from them can be 15 to 20 yards too far. If you can put yourself on the fish, then that's almost all of the battle.

On the other hand, if I'm struggling and haven't seen any signs of fish I'd look to spend at least a couple of hours in one

area, on a well-stocked venue that is. I would remove the back leads and fish for line bites to see if there's anything in the area.

If I started getting liners I would try fishing a bit shorter and change the baits and keep working at it until I got a take. If I wasn't getting any liners and that particular area of the lake seemed completely dead, then I would move and I'd keep moving until I found them.

This is why it's so vital to stay mobile. If you see a carp in a different area of the lake and haven't seen anything in your swim, then move. Take as little kit as you can, so you don't become bogged down, and ensure that you are able to move quickly and easily. Fine down all of your kit and only take what you need. Obviously, you need to be warm, so take enough clothing and your tea-making kit and stay warm all day. Don't forget that you can always take more than you need and leave some in your car.

The tactics outlined in this feature were this stunning winter twenty's downfall. Give 'em a go.

# JACKO'S WINTER TIPS

It's cold out there and bites are hard to come by, so we asked carp-catching ace LEE JACKSON to show you 16 ways to catch more carp this winter.

## 1 PICK YOUR VENUE

A great deal of winter success is down to choosing the right venue. Pick a well-stocked water that continues to be fished by other anglers throughout the colder months. Regular introduction of bait should keep carp searching for food and the disturbance that anglers create should keep the fish moving about regularly.

## 2 CHECK THE MARGINS

Don't neglect the margins, especially if there's bankside cover. Carp will often seek shelter under overhanging trees and bushes and in snags. The shallower water in the edge will warm up far quicker than the rest of the lake.

## 3 FINE DOWN

Fine down your end tackle. There's no need to take things to the extreme, but a size 8 or 10 hook with an 8lb or 10lb mono hooklength is all that you need for winter success. Keep your rigs simple too. Bites can be few and far between, so you don't want to lessen you chances further by using a tangled rig.

## 4 GO NATURAL

Natural baits catch carp all year round, but they really come into their own during winter. A bunch of maggots on the hook coupled with a PVA bag of the little wrigglers will get you plenty of bites. Most people seem to use red maggots, but I've had a lot of success with white/natural-coloured ones.

## 5 QUALITY OVER QUANTITY

Select good winter bait. If you choose to use boilies, then pick one with a good winter track record. Some bait, such as Solar FrostBYT, have been developed specifically for use in cold water, so they're an ideal winter bait. Richworth Tutti Frutti and Nash Scopex Squid Liver Plus are also well worth a go and have caught literally thousands of winter carp.

## 6 TIP YOUR BAIT

A piece of hi-viz artificial corn will add masses of visual attraction to your hook bait. It might just be enough to get an otherwise uninterested carp to pick up your bait.

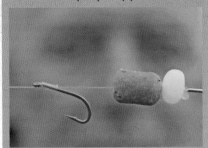

## 7 GO SMALL

Don't use masses of bait. Tiny PVA bags filled with small food items such as 3mm pellets are all you need. Nine times out of 10 in winter, carp will eat a small mouthful of food and ignore a big bed of bait.

## 9 BRIGHTEN UP

Hi-attract, single hook baits work in the cold. Use bright-coloured baits and recast them regularly until you find the carp. On heavily stocked waters, single pieces of hi-viz artificial corn work well – I can't explain why, they just do.

## 8 CAST AT SHOWING FISH

Don't ignore any visual signs that might be caused by carp. Swirls, bubbling, crashing fish and head and shouldering will all tell you where the carp are hiding and are well worth casting at. Sometimes bubbling can be caused by gasses rising from the lake bed, but if you're unsure then cast at it; it might just have been caused by a carp.

## 10 SHOW YOUR SENSITIVE SIDE

Use a sensitive indication set-up. Lightweight bobbins and slack lines are my choice. It also helps if the sensitivity on your alarms can be adjusted. Don't always expect screaming runs in winter, a few bleeps might be the only indications that you get.

## 11 WATCH YOUR FEET!

This might sound a little strange, but when you're sitting waiting for a bite rest your feet on your unhooking mat. The extra insulation it provides will keep your feet warmer than if they're resting on the ground.

## 12 BE COMFORTABLE

You have to be comfortable and warm to be able to concentrate on catching carp. Take plenty of warm clothing, tea-making kit and food. Warm clothing and regular hot drinks will help you fish effectively, even when it's bitterly cold.

## 13 WINTER WINNERS!

If all else fails, try these – Solar's Jacko Pops. They are made from a recipe that I was using for years, way before I gave it to Solar, and have enjoyed massive success with these at all times of year.

## 14 NOTE IT DOWN

Take notes. Keep a record of where and when you catch a winter carp. These notes will enable you to locate hotspots and bite times that'll lead to you being a more efficient and successful winter angler. Don't throw them away once winter's over. Your notes will give you a head start next year, providing that you fish the same lake.

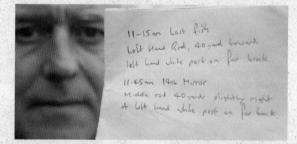

## 16 MAKE EVERY SECOND COUNT

Time is limited on day sessions in winter, so make the most of the time you have. Get to the water at first light, if not before, and fish through until it gets dark. By spending an extra hour or so by the water you might just nick an extra bite in the dark?

## 15 CHOOSE YOUR AREA

Shallow lakes respond very quickly to rising temperatures and even a sunny day can warm the water enough to make the carp feed. But bear in mind that a sudden cold snap will cool the water quickly and could kill the action.

# ANOTHER DIRTY WEEKEND?

**STRATOS 12000E**

**NEW! FOR 2008**

**£199.99**

**STRATOS FS 12000E**
GRAPHITE

**STRATOS 12000E**
GRAPHITE

**£159.99**

The new Fox Stratos 12000E is a true workhorse, a Big Pit reel that simply won't let you down. Made from a tough Graphite Body and utilising the awesome Stratos 12000 technology that made the Stratos MAG such a success, the 12000E is set to become a firm favourite with carp anglers around the world.

- Amazing line lay for distance casting
- Front Clutch Grit Guard
- Freespool on FS 12000E reel
- 13 Ball Bearings on 12000E
- 16 Ball Bearings on FS 12000E
- Oversized Roller Bearing

**For more information visit www.foxint.com**

# PVA
# In Winter

Many anglers believe that PVA is best used during the warmer months, but not ALI HAMIDI. He uses it all year round and, here, he offers some of his top winter PVA tips to help you do the same and catch…

I can imagine how daunting it must be for newcomers to our beloved sport because there are so many different methods, rigs and baits. I take part in every exhibition in the UK for Korda, and some abroad. Consequently, much of my time is spent with top carp angler Dave Gawthorn on the PVA section of our stand. Even after so many years, we are still inundated with questions about getting the best from Funnel Web systems and PVA in general.

We have to thank Steve Spurgeon for innovating the idea of the Funnel Web system during his time at Korda and it's a topic that fascinates a lot of people. For many it's a step too far and it tries people's patience. That's a real shame, because in the past I have explained that not using PVA is like deliberately trying to not catch fish – that's how strongly I feel about the subject.

There are numerous ways of turning a slow session into a red-letter day simply by using PVA effectively. There is such an array of tips and ways of using it that you could probably write a book on the subject. Over the next few pages I'm going to cover a selection of methods that I use to great effect and ones that I feel will maximise your chances of enjoying great sessions, in a host of differing conditions.

## 1 MEATY FISH STICKS

This is arguably one of the best PVA methods that I have used in the past couple of years. After a fair bit of testing by all the boys in Team Korda, the tuna, pellet and groundbait combo has been truly phenomenal. We have all used different tinned fish to great effect – sardines, mackerel and tuna have all performed admirably and, more recently, we have started to experiment with a few other varieties. However, for a 'killer' winter stick mix, try the following.

Place the contents of a tin of tuna into a bait tub. It's important that you use tuna in brine (salty water). The weather has taken a turn for the worse, with the lake now half frozen, so oily baits are out of the question. I've decided to use tuna. Compared to mackerel and sardines, it contains a lot less oil, and coupled with the brine it's a perfect, water-soluble winter ingredient.

Next, add a few handfuls of Halibut Marine pellets – they have a much better release rate than other pellets during winter. Finally, include Bait-Tech Voodoo groundbait, which is meaty. Add this until you take the dampness away from the tuna, otherwise it will melt your PVA; a few handfuls normally suffice.

You will now have a lovely meaty stick mix that will produce the goods, even in the most adverse of conditions.

### CREATE THE MEATY FISH STICK

**1** Place some tinned tuna into a bait box and stir it to break it up.

**2** Add 3mm halibut pellets to enhance the fishy aroma.

**3** Voodoo groundbait is another great addition. It fizzes on the lake bed.

**4** Now mix the concoction until it has a sticky consistency.

**5** Place the stick mix into some Longchuck PVA and compress, like so.

**6** Now thread your hooklength through the middle. Job done!

## 2 THE CHOP BAG

I love fishing with boilies but using them can be a bit one dimensional, especially if you only stick to little round balls. One simple, but effective, way of getting your baits working more effectively is to chop them up in the palm of your hand.

This has two main advantages that should never be overlooked. The first is that when you crack open a boilie it increases the release of flavours. I'm using the new Cell from Mainline, which is one of the best boilies I have ever used. It has a wonderful, creamy, nutty aroma that makes it perfect all year round. A bag of chops will really get the taste buds of the semi-dormant winter carp going.

The other underestimated advantage is that you're making them a little more inconspicuous.

Carp come across round boilies every day and they associate them with danger, so the chopped baits can prevent them becoming used to only picking up round ones. As a consequence, they find it harder to distinguish between the hook bait and freebies, making them easier to fool!

### GIVE 'EM SOME CHOPS

**1** Carefully chop up some whole Mainline Cell boilies.

**2** Place them into a bag and use your thumb to keep it mega-tight.

**3** Tie off with a couple of overhand knots and there you have it!

Ali does battle at dusk.

### 3 HALVED-BAIT STRINGER

I use a lot of small baits throughout winter to counteract the slow, lazy feeding of carp. Large baits are a little too blatant for my liking and will often alert the fish to danger. During the last 15 years, one method that has always stayed at the top of my winter-tricks list is the halved-bait stringer with 10mm baits. I then use one whole 10mm and one half of a 10mm boilie on the hair. It's something a little different from the norm and will often fool wary fish.

This is another wonderful method because the long line of bait gives you a slightly different spread to the concentrated pile of bait that the Korda Funnel Web bag produces. This method is excellent on its own when casting around and exploring the water in front of you, and when fished among a handful of freebies.

## FORM THE HALVED-BAIT STRINGER!

**1** Place 12 or 13 halved boilies onto a long stringer needle.

**2** Use 12 inches of PVA tape because it doesn't slip like PVA string does.

**3** Fold the PVA tape in half and place it in the needle's clasp.

**4** Thread the chops onto the tape, leaving a loop at the top.

**5** Make sure that the loop is large enough to fit over the hook point.

**6** Push the hook point through and tie off the remaining tag end.

### 4 SOLID PVA BAG

The solid bag has probably produced more big fish for me than any other method. Some of my most memorable big-fish captures on weedy and silty lakes have been while using solid bags. With the lead, hooklength and bait all in there together, you have a method that will crash through blanket weed and settle gently on silty lake beds, thereby providing you with a perfect presentation.

I use a drop-off inline set-up on a Safe Zone leader, coupled with the Supernatural braided hook link. This obviously takes a lot longer to set-up than the Korda Funnel Web system, which is why I favour it for more specialised situations, such as when I'm fishing in weed beds or looking to cast a long way. By making it the aerodynamic shape that I have, it's easy to cast this little bag of goodness a very long way because you're making a streamlined, top-heavy system that will cut through the air beautifully. So, for those of you fishing weedy lakes with lower stocks, learn to use solid bags – they are truly devastating.

Ali's tactics prove fruitful, even under the ice.

## FORMING THE SOLID PVA BAG

**1** Place your hook bait in the bottom of the PVA and quarter fill the bag.

**2** Continue to fill with your stick mix and then place the inline lead in the top.

**3** Now, carefully fill the remainder of the bag and twist the top.

**4** Tie off with PVA tape, push in the corners and stick them down using saliva.

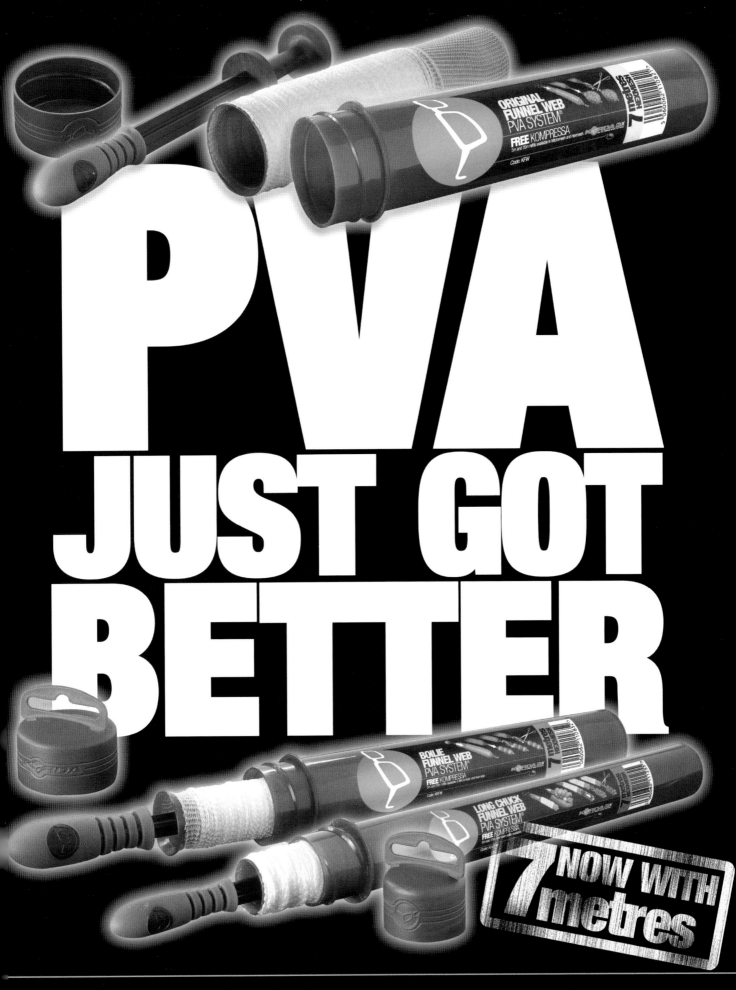

## 5 LIQUID BAG

One very important thing to bear in mind while employing this method is the depth that you use it in. In depths of three feet or less this approach doesn't quite work so well. This is because the liquid doesn't disperse so effectively as it does in deeper water.

So why is this such a good method? Basically, a lot of fish spend time in the upper layers of the water in winter, seldom visiting the bottom. By using the liquid bag you are releasing a lot of water-soluble attraction up through the water column, which is enough to encourage fish to home in on your hook bait.

I rarely use oils in these bags. I favour the water-soluble dips from Mainline or Hinders – these do not melt PVA and are far more effective in winter. Oils congeal in the cold and do not have the same leakage rate. This method has caught me a lot of fish in the worst of conditions, including sweltering-hot summer days and bitterly cold winter days like today, when you have more chance of pulling Jo Guest than a carp down to your bait.

It's very easy to tie – simply keep the bag open with two fingers, then gently pour the dip in until the bag is half full. Now lick the top of the bag and fold over, making sure to leave a bit of bag overlapping to one side. This is where you will hook your bait onto the system.

### THE LIQUID BAG

Pour liquid, oil-based glug into a solid PVA bag, like so.

Hold the PVA bag between your fingers and prepare to lick.

Lick the top of the bag and fold over, leaving the corner free.

Your bag should now look like this. Be careful not to burst it.

Now, carefully pierce the bag with a fine-wired baiting needle.

Finally, nick the hook through the corner flap and you're ready to go!

## 6 SWEETCORN BAG

Very few baits have the track record of sweetcorn in winter. However, on its own it has too much water in it, which means that it melts PVA. A small bag of sweetcorn, coupled with a couple of grains (real or fake) on the hair is a deadly method.

Making sweetcorn PVA friendly is simple. Firstly, drain the water out the tin. Next, pour half the contents into a bait tub. Now glaze the corn in 10ml to 15ml of Hinders Sweetcorn liquid; that's all you need to do. The corn can now be tied in a Funnel Web bag with no fear of melting the PVA. Give it a go; it's a real winner.

### GET ON THE CORN

Empty the juice from the sweetcorn. This will melt the PVA.

Place the grains into a bait tub and cover with Liquid Sweetcorn.

Leave them to soak and then place them into a mesh bag – sorted!

## 7 TYING YOUR CLIP OFF WITH PVA

Some of you will not be used to stopping the lead before it hits the surface. This generally jolts the lead forward when using a PVA bag and prevents the lead clip from dropping the lead. However, I can imagine how frustrating it can be for many of you if you repeatedly lose leads on cast. The last thing that I want you to do is push the tail rubber on too far and potentially make the lead system unsafe – so try this.

Have the tail rubber pushed over three to four teeth on the clip. Then, between there and where the clip dips down, tie some PVA string or tape tightly around the perimeter of the clip, as shown in the picture.

This will be enough to resist the force of the cast and should keep your lead, saving you a few quid in the process! However, when using Funnel Web bags, do try your best to stop the lead before it lands and feel the cast down.

### TYING YOUR LEAD OFF

I use a safety-clip system but only push the tail rubber on lightly so the lead can eject.

To prevent the lead ejecting on impact with the water I tie PVA tape around the clip.

Action can be manic if you apply PVA correctly.

## 8 PELLET BAG

This is where it all started with the Funnel Web. A small parcel of pellets is packed tightly into the Funnel Web system and then hooked on and cast out. You can never underestimate how good this is.

For those of you who haven't used PVA before, I suggest that you try this – just to see how many extra fish it puts on the bank. Try low-oil pellets in winter and high-oil in summer. The key is to use no bigger than 50p-piece-sized bags.

Something that you should always remember is that you're not trying to feed 'em, you're trying to catch 'em!

**Try pellets in PVA – carp love them!**

## 10 A FUNNEL WEB BAG TIED TO A LEAD

For those who don't want to mess about using solid bags, try this. It's ideal when casting tight to snags or weed beds, where you don't want hook links flailing around. Simply tie your Funnel Web bag up and then thread some braid through the holes. Use these tag ends to tie the bag to the swivel on the lead, using a few granny knots. Now hook your bait on and you're ready to go.

### THE WEED BAG!

**1** Create a bag of chops and thread braid through the middle.

**2** Attach the bag to the lead by tying off with a few granny knots.

**3** Now nick your hook point into the bag and it's job done!

## 9 TYING YOUR HAIR AND LEAD OFF WITH PVA

This is simple but very important. A badly presented rig is as good as a lost fish or no bite at all. During the cast the hair can easily wrap around the hook, deeming the rig set-up ineffective. By tying the hair off with PVA tape you are eliminating the chance of this happening. This is of priceless importance.

### TYING YOUR HAIR OFF

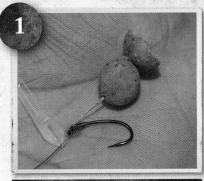

**1** Wrap a 3in section of PVA tape around the hair, trapping it against the hook.

**2** This will prevent the hair from tangling on the cast.

## 11 DIPPING BAGS IN LIQUID

Similarly to the liquid bag, dipping your Funnel Web system in a liquid of your choice releases a phenomenal amount of attraction with very little food. It's very simple and very effective. It's little changes like this that can make all the difference in winter.

Remember, carp are semi-dormant and not in total hibernation. The fishing can be in spurts of intense activity, so make sure that you have something on that will pull the fish down. However, don't soak your bags too far in advance of the cast because the liquid will dissolve into the PVA and prevent the bag from melting.

**Dip your bag for optimum attraction.**

# COLD-WATER CARPING

As the leaves begin to fall and temperatures drop, anglers think that carp stop feeding. They don't and DAVE LANE shows you how to keep catching throughout the colder months.

A rare achievement these days – a carp in the snow. This is my mate Clive Percival at Dinton Pastures.

High pressure and a full, winter moon – not exactly conducive to catching carp!

Throughout this feature I'm going to talk about surviving the cold weather without having to spend long nights and cold days watching icicles forming on your motionless indicators.

Various factors will help you to succeed throughout this period and location really comes into its own at this time.

Unlike during the summer months the fish will tend to spend much longer in specific areas, maybe not moving very far for weeks on end.

Identifying these areas, and establishing an acceptable bait in them, is a sure way of ensuring continued success. In fact, because the areas are more predictable and the feeding times so much more reliable and precise, winter fishing can sometimes become easier than during summer; or at least a lot more rewarding for the time actually spent with baits in the water.

Bait is not the only way to crack the problems of winter fishing. Be aware that the fish can only eat so much food during winter. So, if someone is already baiting all the good winter spots it becomes counterproductive to add yet more food to the equation.

To some extent, baiting for winter can rely on the amount of anglers dropping off dramatically as the temperature falls.

I look at winter fishing from two totally different angles. The first is purely location based and involves the use of single attractor baits placed in the correct spots at the right times of day. I have caught hundreds of winter carp using this method and I've actually caught consistently throughout winter without feeding any free offerings whatsoever!

Quite why they keep picking up hook baits without gaining any sustenance is beyond me, but the fact that they do has been enough to keep me persevering with the method.

Over at Linch Hill one winter I caught fish almost every morning between 11 and 11.30am on a single piece of plastic corn topped with a red plastic maggot. The only feed I used was an occasional spod of maggots at the start of winter, but I soon let this slip and the results stayed the same.

The spots were far more important than the bait and I had 90 per cent of the bites on one rod cast to a very precise little spot next to an old weed bed.

This hit-and-run style of fishing can be very productive, but I still prefer to establish a feeding area, bait and method of my own. This will give a more long-term result and, if done properly, can provide the lion's share of all the fish caught on a lake during the entire winter period.

It's always a good idea to plan your baiting campaign well before winter actually arrives. By the time the leaves begin to fall you should have already started laying plans.

Starting a baiting campaign in the depths of winter is often far too late to get the fish interested in feeding again and fish left to their own devices may well lapse into a semi-torpid state when the water temperatures start to plummet.

It's a lot better to start at a time when the carp are naturally still active and on the look out for food. With a concerted effort you can extend their feeding period well into the colder months.

Unless fish find a readily available food supply during November they can quite often take the easy option of conserving energy by not moving around. This will therefore lower their need for food until the light levels change in February and the fish naturally feed again.

Bait choice is very important if you want to keep getting a return for your efforts and I favour a bait that has a fast breakdown during summer but low levels of oil. If you have a good, established bait that goes mouldy very quickly in high temperatures then there is a fair chance that it will still be giving off the correct signals in the colder months.

I would definitely avoid shelf-life baits or rock-hard, long-lasting baits for any sort of a winter campaign. Good-quality boilies with a proven track record will always win in the end.

Throughout October and early November I'm always happy to bait the entire lake, as the fish are still active and using most of the summer areas; if only occasionally. During late November and December, though, I concentrate the bait into areas that are producing fish, ignoring the more extreme sections that haven't seen any action for a while.

Getting the bait ready for a winter campaign.

This Linch Hill twenty came when the daytime temperature was minus 2°C.

Baiting levels have to be looked at in some detail and will depend upon the stock levels, nuisance fish and, very importantly, the level of bird life. Birds treat bait as a very welcome supplement to a seasonally declined food supply during winter. Coots and mallards are a problem on shallow lakes, but tufties are the real problem, regardless of the depth of water that you are fishing in. Tufted diving birds that arrive here from colder climates during our winter months can eat an incredible amount of boiled baits. They can also hold their breath for an eternity, making sure that they always find something to eat every time that they dive.

along and decide to feed. It's far better to put in half a kilo of bait every evening, just after dark, than to bait with 3kg or 4kg once a week.

Even when you have a bait and area established it can be a mistake to forget about the rest of the lake. Fish can turn up in the strangest places once the water temperatures stabilise later in winter. In fact, they are often seen in the shallows under a layer of ice during January and February!

Years ago carp fishing was abandoned after about November and it was a revelation when a few die-hard anglers proved that carp could be caught whatever the temperatures.

Both of these facts are true, of course, but I think that it has an adverse effect on the fishing rather than a positive one in certain lakes. Once a deep water has reached its winter low in the temperature stakes, it will be affected very little by rising temperatures and gain small benefit from nice, sunny, winter days, or warm low-pressure fronts. Also, there seems to be a fluctuation in temperature at different depths and it's possible that the most comfortable layer of water is seldom at the bottom, where the food is.

This can lead to fish spending vast amounts of time in mid-water, utilising the higher temperature of the trapped layer of water to keep warm.

Fish in this state are very hard to tempt without the use of zig rigs fished at varying heights.

I know of many fish caught as high as 10 feet from the bottom in 12 feet of water during a hard frost, but this does not help us much with a baiting campaign!

If I could pick the perfect water for winter angling it would have varying depths but large areas of shallow water, particularly sheltered areas in the lee of islands and tree-lined banks.

I would bait the mid to lower-depth ranges for continued feeding and watch the shallower water like a hawk, waiting for the first signs of cruising, bubbling or rolling fish.

Shallow water in winter can be approached like summer stalking and a few hours work in the warmest part of the day can turn a blank session on its head with a couple of quick bites.

So where do you choose to put all your time, bait and effort?

## WE ALL BELIEVED THAT DEEPER WATERS WOULD FISH BETTER IN THE COLD.

I work along the lines that approximately a quarter of the bait may stay there long enough to be on offer to the carp. Obviously, the more often you introduce the bait, the more chance it has of still being there when the fish come

Then, for a while, we all believed that deeper waters would fish better in the cold; the theory being that the deep water would take longer to cool and stay at a more stable temperature throughout the cold months.

Occasionally, I'd have the odd friend round!

Learn to read the conditions.

Previous knowledge of winter areas is obviously going to be a massive help because fish are definitely creatures of habit. However, with the use of bait you can actually influence the areas to some degree, but only if you start before they fall into their own routine.

I would pick a couple of spots to start with. One of these would definitely be at the south or west side of the lake so that it is guaranteed to receive a good deal of sunlight on the water. The arc of the sun in winter is very low and a tree-lined eastern bank may see next to no sunlight, leaving it dark and cold for the majority of the day.

Sometimes it really is like endurance fishing.

Keep an eye out for breaks in the weather.

Sheltered spots near to islands can be productive in the right conditions, but these are usually single-bait areas for high-pressure sunny days when the fish are in the upper layers.

For a baiting-up spot I would investigate the actual lake bed in a bit more detail, dragging a big lead through and seeing what is out there.

Silty spots close to underwater features are always good, or sunken snags in deep water, because these areas offer some point of interest for the fish to hold up against. It's incredible just how much of a draw a single branch or tiny old weed bed can offer to fish in the winter.

I know that there will be people who disagree with this statement but, in general, I have found softer lake bed near to gravel and sand to be more productive during winter than fishing on the hard, gravelly ground. I suppose that firm sections of the bottom of the lake – hard clay patches for example – would be the ideal areas.

The other spots I'd consider would be at the northern end of the lake for those times when an easterly or northerly wind sends freezing-cold air into the first area.

Rather than fish on the wind during winter I try to get onto the back of it and fish in the most sheltered areas possible. If you take a slow walk around a lake in winter you will notice that some areas are a lot colder than others, particularly when you turn a corner and find yourself heading into the wind. Small, sheltered, sunny spots are a welcome break on a cold day and can seem almost spring-like by comparison. This is how I envisage the carp looking at the lake during certain conditions, and sitting in the teeth of a biting cold northeasterly wind is the last place I'd expect to find them!

There are many variables to take into account before you pick your spots for baiting. Nevertheless, always remember that you are not working alone when you try and figure it all out. If you spend enough time watching and waiting then the fish will eventually give you all the help you need.

Carp roll, bubble and sometimes leap over their favourite areas and, even in the depths of winter, one little sign can give the game away.

At Dinton one year I caught a 40lb mirror in November by casting at a

In the summer, make a note of where the weed is.

This was a cup of water, INSIDE my bivvy!

It could still happen at any time.

Even the wildlife look on in disbelief sometimes.

single, carpy-looking bubble. The bite came so quickly that I'd only just put the rod back in the rests!

It's not just temperature or wind direction that will affect the fish either, I think that the air pressure plays a far more important role than we realise. High-pressure systems may bring finer weather but the fish seem to respond by rising in the water and becoming harder to tempt on deep-water spots. I don't mean that low pressure is necessarily the only time that you'll catch, because I've had some excellent winter multiple catches in very high pressure.

Maybe it's more a case of rising or falling pressure, or even what part of the lake or specific depths we fish in certain barometric conditions. Whatever the answer, it can't hurt to keep a few notes and, if a good session is had, look out for similar conditions in the same areas in the future.

Hopefully, you will sort out a few likely areas and have some sort of action from them. Keeping the bait going in and not losing your resolve, will definitely help you during December and January. Just because the results might not be fantastic throughout November does not mean that the plan isn't working.

I have found November to be one of the worst months of the year and the fishing can often improve dramatically once the temperatures stabilise a bit as the winter settles in.

The result of a well-timed two-hour session.

This one came after a concerted baiting campaign.

# ZIGGING...
# WITH MAGGOTS!

CRAIG WADDINGTON reveals his revolutionary new tactic to catch late-winter and early spring carp. Give it a try, it's deadly!

I'm angling at Manor Farm in Biggleswade. I arrived yesterday evening to find pretty awful conditions. We're just on the end of a real cold snap, which has made the fishing difficult during the past few weeks. I did a quick circuit of the lake to see if I could unearth any carp activity, but all to no avail. The lake was flat calm, so fish spotting wouldn't have been a problem. I always look for carp before settling in a swim because fish location is paramount, especially at this time of year.

Due to the poor conditions and lack of activity, I eventually settled in a swim that possesses a proven track record during winter. I've caught many carp from that area, even when half the lake was frozen, so it was to be the ideal spot. Firstly, I set up all three rods and boated them out to some of the known hotspots that I remembered from previous sessions.

At around 40-yards range there is a reasonably clear spot, located in a surrounding weed bed. It's a cracking spot because carp often hold up in the weed in tight shoals to keep warm during the cold snap. If there is a bait placed close by then you never know, they might just be tempted to feed. Carp also feed on the dying weed because they can often find enough food and organisms to keep their metabolism up. As I set sail with my bait boat towards the area I saw a carp break the surface, followed by another shortly afterwards. I didn't think they were particularly big, but they were active and that kept my confidence high.

With the carp obviously moving, I felt that I'd keep my options open by fishing a small pop-up on the first rod and zig

rigs on the remaining two. I've had a lot of success using zig rigs during winter, and even more so when they're showing like they have done. With the first bait dropped I set about casting the two zigs. I'm never too worried how accurate the zig rigs land because they sit at whatever depth you alter them to. As long as they're not in thick weed I'm happy and at this time of year when the weed has died back it's not a problem.

I then introduced some free bait over the top of the zigs with the bait boat. This included a mixture of maggots, both live and dead, and a few handfuls of pellets featuring various buoyancies.

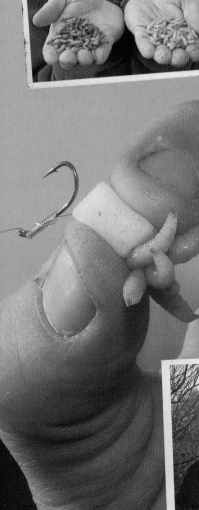

I like to give the carp a mixture of live and dead maggots...

... because the dead ones sink a lot slower.

I like to use dead and live maggots so that the carp are finding baits of different consistencies. The live maggots flutter through the water levels with movement, hopefully attracting the carp as they wriggle down to the lake bed. Conversely, the dead maggots sink extremely slowly and often hang around at mid-water before sinking to the bottom. This will attract carp to your zig rig because they seek slow-sinking food items.

Many anglers think that winter carp hold up tight to the lake bed, and to a certain degree they are correct. However, if you get a slight change in temperature, or pressure, sometimes they'll move higher in the water. I believe it has something to do with the thermoclines, but I won't go into that now.

With the traps set I erected the bivvy and organised myself for the long night ahead. Winter nights can be an energy-draining experience so I always take a radio to keep me sane and a kettle to ensure that my body temperature remains comfortable. If you're cold your mind won't be on fishing and will let you down in the long run. I made myself a piping-hot cup of tea and sat on my bedchair awaiting action.

The night began to draw on and eventually I hit the sack, hoping for the wake-up call of a screaming alarm.

The night passed all too quickly and at 7am, as the sun began to appear, I received a twitchy bite on my middle rod. The bobbin lifted to the top, then dropped to the floor and rose again. This time it stayed tight against the rod, indicating a proper take. I forced the zip of my sleeping bag open, climbed into my boots and legged it towards the rod. It was absolutely freezing and there were patches of frost on my reel and rod from the Arctic temperatures. The adrenaline rush that goes through your body when being awoken by an alarm is immense, though, and all thoughts of the cold were immediately forgotten.

What carp could resist this?

The bait boat helps me to pinpoint my chosen spots.

I lifted into whatever was attached and played it carefully in the open water. The small hook held firm and following a short scrap I netted the first carp of the session. It was only small but more than welcome in such dismal conditions.

I lifted the little common onto my mat and began to remove the successful rig. It had taken the zig rig that was coupled with maggots. The fish was then carefully returned to the crystal-clear water and I recast to the same spot, armed with fresh maggot hook baits. I followed this with another bait boat holding a mixture of baits and jumped back into the bag.

The night was pretty slow and as I'm opening my eyes I only have that one carp to my name. Because I've only received the one take I'm reeling in my other zig rig to check if the maggots are okay. They are all intact and, to be honest, I'm surprised that I haven't received anything else. At least I have had a bite, though, and I'm hugely grateful because the night-time conditions were completely against me.

It was the maggots that helped me do the business. I've caught so many carp using them on the zig rig when all else fails. The carp take the bait out of sheer curiosity and the movement induces them into taking it. The fish are used to seeing boilies day in, day out and it's the little differences that can pay dividends.

To pop the maggots up off the lead I simply tie them onto a small ring that is attached to a sliver of foam. This is extremely buoyant and will stay popped

As the sun makes an appearance I anticipate some action.

## HOW TO TIE CRAIG'S MAGGOT ZIG RIG

**1** These are the components that you'll need to tie the rig. The foam is vital.

**2** Strip off the required length of mono. I like the zig rig to sit just under the surface.

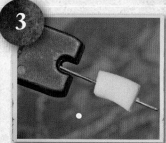

**3** Trim off a rectangular piece of yellow foam and thread a baiting needle through it.

**4** Place the mono onto the needle by doubling it over and pull it through the foam.

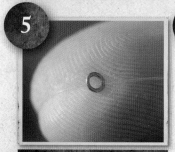

**5** Place a 2mm rig ring onto the mono, like so. Don't drop it, though, because it's tiny!

**6** Now tie the ring on with a simple four-turn blood knot. Moisten and then pull tight.

**7** You then need to ease the foam back towards the ring and pull the knot inside.

**8** Thread your hook down the mono and create a knotless knot tight to the shank.

**9** Thread several maggots onto a sewing needle. This prevents them bursting.

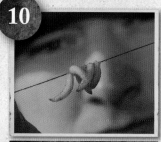

**10** Slowly push six or seven maggots onto some black cotton, but do it carefully.

**11** Put one end of the cotton through the ring and tie on with five granny knots.

**12** Pull the knot securely, trim the tag ends and you're ready to go. Superb!

up forever. I don't think you need to go over the top on the amounts of maggots either; eight or nine should suffice.

One important thing that you need to note when zig rigging maggots is to feed correctly. To successfully fish zig rigs you need to persuade the carp to compete in the upper layers of the water. The only way to do this is to feed and create a level of food where the bait drifts around and induces the carp to rise from the lake bed. This is why it's important to choose baits of different buoyancies. You want some to sink, some of neutral buoyancy that just drift around and others to sink slowly through the water levels.

This method has worked at nearly every venue that I've fished, but I don't only use maggots. Sometimes in the clear, cold water a bright-coloured pop-up will score well, as will a piece of coloured foam fished on its own. Black foam can be a cracking artificial

bait and, believe it or not, it can work a treat during the hours of darkness, too. It could be to do with the silhouette against the moonlit sky or any number of other things. We will never know, but if it catches carp then it is good enough for me.

The rest of the day went pretty slow and I only managed another small common of a couple of pounds. Again it was caught on the zig-rigged maggots, so it proves my point. The only two bites I received both came to the maggots and the bottom bait remained untouched!

The maggot zig works all year round.